The
BUMPER
BOOK of
SPORTING
WIT

THE BUMPER BOOK OF SPORTING WIT

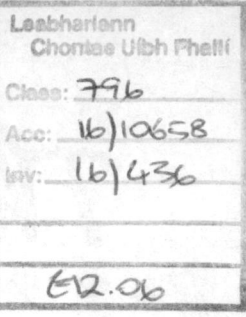
Summersdale Publishers Ltd
46 West Street
Chichester
West Sussex
PO19 1RP
UK

www.summersdale.com

Printed and bound in the Czech Republic

ISBN: 978-1-84953-917-3

Substantial discounts on bulk quantities of Summersdale books are available to corporations, professional associations and other organisations. For details contact Nicky Douglas by telephone: +44 (0) 1243 756902, fax: +44 (0) 1243 786300 or email: nicky@summersdale.com.

The BUMPER BOOK of SPORTING WIT

Richard Benson

summersdale

CONTENTS

EDITOR'S NOTE

Sport gives us everything, from high drama and huge personalities to classic quips and hilarious gaffes. Whether on grass, snow, canvas or tarmac, at high altitude or racing through water, the triumphs and disasters of the sporting world have led to some golden observations.

Win, lose or draw, players, coaches, fans and commentators have always had something to say. Sometimes their words are profound or just baffling (see Sporting Philosophers on page 43). Sometimes they're silly or saucy (The Rude Bits, page 275). Often they're blunders made when brain and mouth are simply not in sync (How Travel Broadens the Mind, page 56). But it's always entertaining.

As well as these themed sections, you'll find chapters that are specific to your favourite sport. And sprinkled throughout the book there are selections of the best quips and cock-ups from the greats of sporting commentary, from motor racing's Murray Walker to golf's Peter Alliss.

At the end of the day, when the bell goes or the whistle blows – and no matter whether you're a casual spectator or an utter obsessive – there's truly something for everyone in these pages.

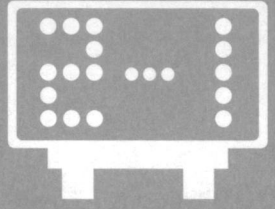

IT'S A NUMBERS GAME

I've got fourteen bookings this season,
eight of which were my fault and
seven of which were disputable.

PAUL GASCOIGNE, ENGLISH FOOTBALLER

· ·

95 PER CENT OF PUTTS WHICH
FINISH SHORT DON'T GO IN.

ROBERT GREEN, BRITISH GOLF WRITER

· ·

Just under 10 seconds for Nigel Mansell.
Call it 9.5 seconds in round numbers.

**MURRAY WALKER, ENGLISH
MOTORSPORT COMMENTATOR**

A VERY SMALL CROWD HERE TODAY.
I CAN COUNT THE PEOPLE ON ONE
HAND. CAN'T BE MORE THAN 30.

**MICHAEL ABRAHAMSON,
SOUTH AFRICAN CRICKET COMMENTATOR**

....

For me to win the Manager of
the Month award I would have to
win nine games out of eight.

NEIL WARNOCK, ENGLISH FOOTBALL MANAGER

....

I WANT TO REACH FOR 150
OR 200 POINTS THIS SEASON,
WHICHEVER COMES FIRST.

DAVID HOLWELL, NEW ZEALAND RUGBY PLAYER

Baseball is 90 per cent mental.
The other half is physical.

YOGI BERRA, AMERICAN BASEBALL PLAYER

. . . .

SOUTHAMPTON HAVE BEATEN
BRIGHTON 3–1. THAT'S A REPEAT
OF LAST YEAR'S RESULT, WHEN
SOUTHAMPTON WON 5–1.

DES LYNAM, ENGLISH SPORTS PRESENTER

. . . .

We're going to turn this team
around 360 degrees.

JASON KIDD, AMERICAN BASKETBALL
PLAYER AND COACH

WE'VE WON ONE ON THE TROT.

ALEC STEWART, ENGLISH CRICKETER

Any time Detroit scores more than 100 points and holds the other team below 100 points, they almost always win.

DOUG COLLINS, AMERICAN BASKETBALL PLAYER AND COACH

MIRANDINHA WILL HAVE MORE SHOTS THIS AFTERNOON THAN BOTH SIDES PUT TOGETHER.

MALCOLM MACDONALD, ENGLISH FOOTBALLER

There were congratulations and high sixes all round.

RICHIE BENAUD,
AUSTRALIAN
CRICKET COMMENTATOR

Kevin Keegan and I have 63 international caps between us. He has 63 of them.

CRAIG BROWN, SCOTTISH FOOTBALL MANAGER

....

HE'S RANKED NUMBER THREE IN BRITAIN, NUMBER FOUR IN THE WORLD. YOU CAN'T GET ANY HIGHER THAN THAT!

JOHN LOWE, ENGLISH DARTS PLAYER

....

They were numerically outnumbered.

GARRY BIRTLES, ENGLISH FOOTBALLER AND PUNDIT

THE AGELESS DENNIS WISE, NOW IN HIS THIRTIES.

MARTIN TYLER, ENGLISH SPORTS PRESENTER

• •

You guys pair up in groups of three, then line up in a circle.

COLIN COOPER, NEW ZEALAND RUGBY COACH

• •

THE LAST TIME IRELAND PLAYED ENGLAND WE BEAT THEM 1–1.

JIM SHERIDAN, IRISH FOOTBALLER

Some of our players can hardly write their own names, but you should see them add up.

KARL-HEINZ THIELEN, GERMAN FOOTBALL MANAGER, REFERRING TO HIS SQUAD'S SAVVINESS REGARDING THEIR SALARIES

....

I WOULD DIE TOMORROW IF I COULD HAVE FIVE MORE YEARS TO PLAY CRICKET FOR YORKSHIRE AND ENGLAND.

GEOFFREY BOYCOTT, ENGLISH CRICKETER AND COMMENTATOR

....

Isolate yourself if you want, but never alone.

CHRISTOPHE PIAZZOLI, FRENCH RUGBY COACH

IRELAND WILL GIVE 99 PER CENT
– EVERYTHING THEY'VE GOT.

MARK LAWRENSON, IRISH FOOTBALLER AND PUNDIT

....

Moses Kiptanui, the 19-year-old Kenyan
who turned 20 a few weeks ago.

DAVID COLEMAN, ENGLISH SPORTS COMMENTATOR

....

AS FOR WAGES, THE PLAYERS HAVE
HAD A TRIM, THE CHAIRMAN
HAS HAD A TRIM, AND I HAVE
HAD A SHORT BACK AND SIDES.

HARRY REDKNAPP, ENGLISH FOOTBALL MANAGER

An inch or two either side of the post
and that would have been a goal.

**DAVE BASSETT, ENGLISH FOOTBALL
MANAGER AND PUNDIT**

• •

A LOVING WIFE IS BETTER THAN
MAKING 50 IN CRICKET, OR EVEN
99. BEYOND THAT I WILL NOT GO.

J. M. BARRIE, SCOTTISH WRITER

• •

Argentina are the second-best
team in the world, and there's
no higher praise than that.

KEVIN KEEGAN, ENGLISH FOOTBALLER AND MANAGER

As with every

YOUNG PLAYER,

HE'S ONLY 18

ALEX FERGUSON,
SCOTTISH FOOTBALL MANAGER

IT'S 50–50 IN WALES' FAVOUR.

**IAN ROBERTSON, SCOTTISH RUGBY PLAYER
AND COMMENTATOR**

If you had to name one person to blame it would have to be the players.

THEO FOLEY, IRISH FOOTBALL MANAGER

I'D FIGHT LLOYD HONEYGHAN FOR NOTHING IF THE PRICE WAS RIGHT.

MARLON STARLING, AMERICAN BOXER

They had a dozen corners,
maybe 12, I'm guessing.

CRAIG BROWN, SCOTTISH FOOTBALL MANAGER

. . . .

YORKSHIRE ALL OUT FOR
232, HUTTON ILL. NO, I'M
SORRY, HUTTON 111.

JOHN SNAGGE, ENGLISH SPORTS COMMENTATOR

. . . .

Ritchie has now scored 11 goals, exactly
double the number he got last season.

ALAN PARRY, ENGLISH FOOTBALL COMMENTATOR

WE MUST HAVE HAD 99 PER
CENT OF THE GAME. IT WAS
THE OTHER 3 PER CENT THAT
COST US THE MATCH.

RUUD GULLIT, DUTCH FOOTBALLER AND MANAGER

A golf course is comprised of 18
holes, 17 of them unnecessary,
but included simply to create the
maximum amount of frustration.

TERRY WOGAN, IRISH TELEVISION PRESENTER

ONE YEAR I PLAYED FOR 15 MONTHS.

**FRANZ BECKENBAUER, GERMAN FOOTBALLER
AND MANAGER**

For years I thought the club's
name was Partick Thistle Nil.

BILLY CONNOLLY, SCOTTISH COMEDIAN

. . . .

IF YOU GO IN WITH TWO FAST
BOWLERS AND ONE BREAKS DOWN,
YOU'RE LEFT TWO SHORT.

BOB MASSIE, AUSTRALIAN CRICKETER

. . . .

England have the best fans in
the world, and Scotland's ones
are also second to none.

KEVIN KEEGAN, ENGLISH FOOTBALLER AND MANAGER

SIMPLY
THE BEST

IF YOU CAN KEEP PLAYING TENNIS WHEN SOMEONE IS SHOOTING A GUN DOWN THE STREET, THAT'S CONCENTRATION!

SERENA WILLIAMS, AMERICAN TENNIS PLAYER, ON LEARNING HER TRADE IN A DEPRIVED NEIGHBOURHOOD

....

The minute you start talking about what you're going to do if you lose, you have lost.

GEORGE SHULTZ, AMERICAN RACING DRIVER

....

WHENEVER PLAYERS DISAGREE WITH ME, WE TALK ABOUT IT FOR 20 MINUTES AND THEN WE DECIDE I WAS RIGHT.

BRIAN CLOUGH, ENGLISH FOOTBALL MANAGER

That lad could throw 180 standing
one-legged in a hammock.

SID WADDELL, ENGLISH DARTS COMMENTATOR

. . . .

I AM THE NUMBER ONE NINJA
AND I HAVE KILLED ALL THE
SHOGUNS BEFORE ME.

SHAQUILLE O'NEAL, AMERICAN BASKETBALL PLAYER

. . . .

Float like a butterfly, sting like a bee. His
hands can't hit what his eyes can't see.

MUHAMMAD ALI, AMERICAN BOXER

I wouldn't say

I WAS THE BEST MANAGER IN THE BUSINESS.

BUT I WAS IN THE TOP ONE.

BRIAN CLOUGH,
ENGLISH FOOTBALL MANAGER

DON'T TOUCH HIM! HE'S A GOD!

GENERAL ANTONELLI, MUSSOLINI'S SPORTS MINISTER, TRYING TO KEEP THE CROWDS AWAY FROM GINO BARTALI AFTER HE WON THE TOUR DE FRANCE IN 1938

· ·

They came to see me bat, not to see you bowl.

W. G. GRACE, ENGLISH CRICKETER, REFUSING TO LEAVE THE CREASE HAVING BEEN BOWLED OUT FIRST BALL

I threw the kitchen sink at him but he went to the bathroom and came back with the tub.

ANDY RODDICK,
AMERICAN TENNIS PLAYER,
ON ROGER FEDERER

THERE ARE 199 WAYS TO GET
BEAT, BUT ONLY ONE WAY
TO WIN; GET THERE FIRST.

WILLIE SHOEMAKER, AMERICAN JOCKEY

····································

I'm undisputed and there's
no disputing that.

LENNOX LEWIS, BRITISH–CANADIAN BOXER

····································

WHOEVER SAID 'IT'S NOT
WHETHER YOU WIN OR LOSE
THAT COUNTS' PROBABLY LOST.

**MARTINA NAVRATILOVA,
CZECH–AMERICAN TENNIS PLAYER**

I done wrestled with an alligator. I done tussled with a whale, handcuffed lightning, thrown thunder in jail. Only last week, I murdered a rock, injured a stone, hospitalised a brick. I'm so mean I make medicine sick.

MUHAMMAD ALI, AMERICAN BOXER

. . . .

HE'S BIGGLES, THE VC, EL ALAMEIN, THE TANK COMMANDER, HE'S EVERYTHING. I MEAN, HOW COULD A SCHOOLBOY NOT WANT TO BE LIKE IAN BOTHAM?

LORD TIM HUDSON, ENGLISH IMPRESARIO

There seems only one way to beat George Foreman: shell him for three days and then send the infantry in.

HUGH McILVANNEY, SCOTTISH SPORTS JOURNALIST

....

JOHN DALY'S DRIVING IS UNBELIEVABLE. I DON'T GO THAT FAR ON MY HOLIDAYS.

IAN BAKER-FINCH, AUSTRALIAN GOLFER

....

I don't suppose I can call you a lucky bleeder when you've got 347.

**ANGUS FRASER, ENGLISH CRICKETER,
TO BRIAN LARA**

ROME WASN'T BUILT IN
A DAY, BUT I WASN'T ON
THAT PARTICULAR JOB.

BRIAN CLOUGH, ENGLISH FOOTBALL MANAGER

· ·

Champions keep playing until they get it right.

BILLIE JEAN KING, AMERICAN TENNIS PLAYER

· ·

I'VE FAILED OVER AND OVER
AND OVER AGAIN IN MY LIFE,
AND THAT IS WHY I SUCCEED.

MICHAEL JORDAN, AMERICAN BASKETBALL PLAYER

TALKING
ABSOLUTE
BALLS

All the reds are in the open
now, apart from the blue.

**JOHN VIRGO, ENGLISH SNOOKER PLAYER
AND COMMENTATOR**

· ·

PART OF THE ART OF BOWLING
SPIN IS TO MAKE THE BATSMAN
THINK SOMETHING SPECIAL IS
HAPPENING WHEN IT ISN'T.

SHANE WARNE, AUSTRALIAN CRICKETER

· ·

Strut must be happy to see that ball
struggle on and die as short as a carrot.

HARRY RIGBY, ENGLISH BOWLS COMMENTATOR

RUGBY IS A GAME FOR THE
MENTALLY DEFICIENT. WHO ELSE
BUT AN ENGLISHMAN COULD
INVENT AN OVAL BALL?

PETER POOK, ENGLISH WRITER

. . . .

Golf is a fascinating game. It has
taken me nearly forty years to
discover that I can't play it.

TED RAY, ENGLISH COMEDIAN

. . . .

I BOWL SO SLOW THAT IF I DON'T
LIKE THE LOOK OF IT, I CAN RUN
AFTER IT AND BRING IT BACK.

J. M. BARRIE, SCOTTISH WRITER

He's obviously worked out for himself that he doesn't need that last red. Great thinker, this man.

DENNIS TAYLOR, NORTHERN IRISH SNOOKER PLAYER

· ·

HIT THE BALL. FIND THE BALL. REPEAT UNTIL THE BALL IS IN THE HOLE. HAVE FUN. THE END.

CHUCK HOGAN, AMERICAN GOLF INSTRUCTOR

· ·

Ossie Ardiles strokes the ball like it's part of his own anatomy.

JIMMY MAGEE, IRISH SPORTS BROADCASTER

The Croatians don't play well without the ball.

BARRY VENISON,
ENGLISH FOOTBALLER
AND PUNDIT

IT'S GOOD SPORTSMANSHIP TO
NOT PICK UP LOST GOLF BALLS
WHILE THEY ARE STILL ROLLING.

MARK TWAIN, AMERICAN WRITER

· ·

Bums play pool, gentlemen play billiards.

DANIEL McGOORTY, AMERICAN WRITER

· ·

WHY IS THERE ONLY ONE
FOOTBALL FOR 22 PLAYERS? IF YOU
GAVE A BALL TO EACH OF THEM,
THEY'D STOP FIGHTING FOR IT.

ANONYMOUS

And for those of you watching in black and white, the pink is next to the green.

TED LOWE, ENGLISH SNOOKER COMMENTATOR

. . . .

RUGBY IS PLAYED BY MEN WITH ODD-SHAPED BALLS.

CAR BUMPER STICKER

. . . .

Welcome to Worcester, where we have just seen Barry Richards hit one of Basil D'Oliveira's balls clean out of the ground.

BRIAN JOHNSTON, ENGLISH CRICKET COMMENTATOR

....

If you think it's hard to meet

**NEW PEOPLE,
TRY PICKING UP**

THE WRONG
GOLF BALL.

JACK LEMMON, AMERICAN ACTOR

....

WHOEVER CALLED SNOOKER 'CHESS WITH BALLS' WAS RUDE, BUT RIGHT.

CLIVE JAMES, AUSTRALIAN AUTHOR AND PRESENTER

••••••••••••••••••••••••••••••••

I regard golf as an expensive way of playing marbles.

G. K. CHESTERTON, ENGLISH WRITER

••••••••••••••••••••••••••••••••

JOHNNY MILLER GETS BALLS OUT OF THE BUNKER AS SMOOTHLY AS A MAN LIFTING A BREAST OUT OF AN EVENING GOWN.

PHIL HARRIS, AMERICAN ACTOR

SPORTING
PHILOSOPHERS

Sometimes you see beautiful people with no brains. Sometimes you have ugly people who are intelligent, like scientists.

JOSÉ MOURINHO, PORTUGUESE FOOTBALL MANAGER

• •

THE PLACE OF THE FATHER IN THE MODERN SUBURBAN FAMILY IS A VERY SMALL ONE, PARTICULARLY IF HE PLAYS GOLF.

BERTRAND RUSSELL, ENGLISH PHILOSOPHER

• •

I would like to be referred to as 'The Big Aristotle'.

SHAQUILLE O'NEAL, AMERICAN BASKETBALL PLAYER

IT IS ENJOYABLE TO MAKE THINGS VISIBLE THAT ARE INVISIBLE.

ERIC CANTONA, FRENCH FOOTBALLER

● ●

Before you criticise someone, you should run a mile in their shoes. That way, you're a mile away and you have their shoes.

ANONYMOUS

WHEN YOU COME TO A FORK
IN THE ROAD, TAKE IT.

YOGI BERRA, AMERICAN BASEBALL PLAYER

....

You can discover more about a
person in an hour of play than
in a year of conversation.

PLATO, GREEK PHILOSOPHER

....

THE OXFORD ROWING CREW
– EIGHT MINDS WITH BUT A
SINGLE THOUGHT, IF THAT.

MAX BEERBOHM, ENGLISH ESSAYIST

If history is going to repeat itself,
I should think we can expect
the same thing again.

**TERRY VENABLES, ENGLISH FOOTBALLER
AND MANAGER**

· ·

DON'T LOOK BACK. SOMETHING
MIGHT BE GAINING ON YOU.

LEROY 'SATCHEL' PAIGE, AMERICAN BASEBALL PLAYER

· ·

The man who views the world at
50 the same as he did at 20 has
wasted 30 years of his life.

MUHAMMAD ALI, AMERICAN BOXER

JACK CHARLTON'S PHILOSOPHY OF SOCCER WAS, 'IF PLAN A FAILS, TRY PLAN A'.

MARK LAWRENSON, IRISH FOOTBALLER AND PUNDIT

· ·

The English are not very spiritual people, so they invented cricket to give them some idea of eternity.

GEORGE BERNARD SHAW, IRISH PLAYWRIGHT

· ·

THERE ARE NO TRAFFIC JAMS ALONG THE EXTRA MILE.

ROGER STAUBACH, AMERICAN FOOTBALL PLAYER

Luck is what happens when preparation meets opportunity.

DARRELL ROYAL, AMERICAN FOOTBALL COACH

· ·

SMILE WELL AND OFTEN.
IT MAKES PEOPLE WONDER
WHAT YOU'RE UP TO.

LEROY 'SATCHEL' PAIGE, AMERICAN BASEBALL PLAYER

· ·

Depend on the rabbit's foot
if you will, but remember it
didn't work for the rabbit.

R. E. SHAY, AMERICAN HUMORIST

The moral of the story is not to listen to those who tell you not to play the violin but stick to the tambourine.

JOSÉ MOURINHO,
PORTUGUESE
FOOTBALL MANAGER

SOME PEOPLE THINK FOOTBALL IS
A MATTER OF LIFE AND DEATH.
I CAN ASSURE THEM IT IS MUCH
MORE SERIOUS THAN THAT.

BILL SHANKLY, SCOTTISH FOOTBALL MANAGER

· ·

If only Hitler and Mussolini could
have a good game of bowls once a
week at Geneva, I feel that Europe
would not be as troubled as it is.

**R. G. BRISCOE, BRITISH POLITICIAN,
DURING WORLD WAR 2**

I ALWAYS TURN TO THE SPORTS
PAGES FIRST, WHICH RECORD
PEOPLE'S ACCOMPLISHMENTS.
THE FRONT PAGE HAS NOTHING
BUT MAN'S FAILURES.

EARL WARREN, AMERICAN JURIST

. . . .

It is foolish and quite unfitting for
an educated man to spend all his
time on acquiring bulging muscles,
a thick neck and mighty thighs. The
large amounts they are compelled
to eat make them dull-witted.

SENECA, ROMAN PHILOSOPHER

WHEN THE SEAGULLS FOLLOW THE TRAWLER, IT IS BECAUSE THEY THINK SARDINES WILL BE THROWN INTO THE SEA.

ERIC CANTONA, FRENCH FOOTBALLER, ON BEING QUESTIONED ABOUT HIS BAN FOR KICKING A SPECTATOR

....

Victory goes to the player who makes the next-to-last mistake.

SAVIELLY TARTAKOWER, POLISH-FRENCH CHESS PLAYER

....

WINNING ALL THE TIME IS NOT NECESSARILY GOOD FOR THE TEAM.

JOHN TOSHACK, WELSH FOOTBALLER

When stones are
**THROWN AT
YOU, CONVERT**
THEM INTO
MILESTONES.

SACHIN TENDULKAR,
INDIAN CRICKETER

So frivolous is Man that the least thing,
such as playing billiards or hitting a ball,
is sufficient enough to amuse him.

**BLAISE PASCAL, FRENCH POLYMATH
AND PHILOSOPHER**

· ·

IT'S NOT WHETHER YOU WIN
OR LOSE – BUT WHETHER
I WIN OR LOSE.

SANDY LYLE, SCOTTISH GOLFER

· ·

You miss 100 per cent of the
shots you don't take.

**WAYNE GRETZKY, CANADIAN ICE HOCKEY
PLAYER AND COACH**

HOW TRAVEL BROADENS THE MIND

I DO SWEAR A LOT BUT THE
ADVANTAGE OF HAVING PLAYED
ABROAD IS THAT I CAN CHOOSE
A DIFFERENT LANGUAGE
FROM THE REFEREE'S.

JÜRGEN KLINSMANN, GERMAN FOOTBALLER

. . . .

In Russia, if a male athlete loses,
he becomes a female athlete.

YAKOV SMIRNOFF, UKRAINIAN–AMERICAN COMEDIAN

. . . .

ENGLAND AND AMERICA SHOULD
SCRAP CRICKET AND BASEBALL
AND COME UP WITH A NEW GAME
THAT THEY BOTH CAN PLAY.
LIKE BASEBALL, FOR EXAMPLE.

ROBERT BENCHLEY, AMERICAN HUMORIST

If you have a fortnight's holiday in Dublin, you qualify to play for the national side.

MIKE ENGLAND, WELSH FOOTBALLER AND MANAGER

....

WHEN I DROVE FOR BRITISH TEAMS, THEY CALLED ME 'THE TADPOLE' BECAUSE I WAS TOO SMALL TO BE A FROG.

ALAIN PROST, FRENCH RACING DRIVER

....

Born in Italy, most of his fights have been in his native New York.

DES LYNAM, ENGLISH SPORTS PRESENTER

I'VE JUST NAMED THE TEAM I WOULD LIKE TO REPRESENT WALES IN THE NEXT WORLD CUP: BRAZIL.

BOBBY GOULD, ENGLISH FOOTBALLER AND WALES MANAGER

. . . .

I get a kick out of watching him pick up the accent. He's using words like 'brilliant' and 'lovely'.

ANDRE AGASSI, AMERICAN TENNIS PLAYER, ON CANADIAN GREG RUSEDSKI BECOMING BRITISH NO. 1

PINERO HAS MISSED THE
PUTT. I WONDER WHAT HE'S
THINKING IN SPANISH.

RENTON LAIDLAW, SCOTTISH GOLF COMMENTATOR

I've seen batting all over the world.
And in other countries, too.

KEITH MILLER, AUSTRALIAN CRICKETER

OTHER NATIONS HAVE HISTORY.
WE HAVE FOOTBALL.

ONDINO VIERA, URUGUAYAN FOOTBALL MANAGER

I couldn't settle in Italy –

IT WAS LIKE LIVING IN

A FOREIGN COUNTRY.

IAN RUSH, WELSH FOOTBALLER

The Brazilians aren't as good as they
used to be. Or as they are now.

**KENNY DALGLISH, SCOTTISH FOOTBALLER
AND MANAGER**

· ·

IF STALIN HAD LEARNED TO PLAY
CRICKET, THE WORLD MIGHT NOW
BE A BETTER PLACE TO LIVE IN.

ARCHBISHOP OF LIVERPOOL, 1940s

· ·

I'd love to play for one of those
Italian teams, like Barcelona.

MARK DRAPER, ENGLISH FOOTBALLER

PLAYING WITH WINGERS IS MORE
EFFECTIVE AGAINST EUROPEAN
SIDES LIKE BRAZIL THAN
ENGLISH SIDES LIKE WALES.

RON GREENWOOD, ENGLISH FOOTBALL MANAGER

· ·

When I'm batting, I like to
pretend I'm a West Indian.

DARREN GOUGH, ENGLISH CRICKETER

· ·

I DON'T WANT ROONEY TO LEAVE
THESE SHORES, BUT IF HE DOES
I THINK HE'LL GO ABROAD.

IAN WRIGHT, ENGLISH FOOTBALLER

I'm absolutely thrilled and over the world about it.

TESSA SANDERSON,
ENGLISH JAVELIN THROWER

I just want to get into the middle
and get the right sort of runs.

**ROBIN SMITH, SOUTH AFRICAN-BORN
ENGLISH CRICKETER, ON SUFFERING FROM
DIARRHOEA ON TOUR IN INDIA**

• •

TERRY VENABLES COULD DO
A BARCELONA AT LEEDS, LIKE
HE DID AT BARCELONA.

TED BUXTON, ENGLISH FOOTBALL SCOUT

• •

It was strange. The only English words
I saw were Sony and Mitsubishi.

**BILL GULLICKSON, AMERICAN BASEBALL PLAYER,
ON PLAYING IN JAPAN**

TO PLAY HOLLAND YOU HAVE TO PLAY THE DUTCH.

RUUD GULLIT, DUTCH FOOTBALLER AND MANAGER

....

Venezuela! Great, that's the Italian city with the guys in the boats, right?

MURAD MUHAMMAD, AMERICAN BOXING PROMOTER, ON ARRANGING A FIGHT IN SOUTH AMERICA

....

WHEN ENGLAND GO TO TURKEY THERE COULD BE FATALITIES. OR EVEN WORSE, INJURIES.

PHIL NEAL, ENGLISH FOOTBALLER AND MANAGER

San Marino play like men who
expect to encounter visa problems
if they approach the halfway line.

TOM HUMPHRIES, IRISH SPORTS JOURNALIST

. . . .

A REAL IRISH FOOTBALL FAN IS ONE
WHO KNOWS THE NATIONALITY
OF EVERY PLAYER ON THE
REPUBLIC OF IRELAND TEAM.

JACK CHARLTON, ENGLISH FOOTBALLER AND
REPUBLIC OF IRELAND MANAGER

There are so many Latino ball-players, we're going to have to get a Latin instructor up here.

PHIL RIZZUTO, AMERICAN BASEBALL PLAYER

THE POOR BRITISH TEND TO STAND UP STRAIGHT AND TAKE IT ON THE CHOPS, BLEEDING ALMOST BEFORE THE OPENING BELL.

STEPHEN BRUNT, CANADIAN SPORTS JOURNALIST, ON BRITISH BOXERS

It took me five years to learn to spell Chattanooga – and then we moved to Albuquerque.

JOE MORRISON, AMERICAN FOOTBALL COACH

ANYONE
FOR
TENNIS?

HE'S NOW LETTING CHANG PLAY HIS OWN GAME – AND HE DOES THAT BETTER THAN ANYONE.

CHRISTINE TRUMAN JANES, ENGLISH TENNIS PLAYER

....

Diane, keeping her head beautifully on her shoulders.

ANN JONES, ENGLISH TENNIS PLAYER

....

NOBODY BEATS VITAS GERULAITIS 17 TIMES IN A ROW.

VITAS GERULAITIS, AMERICAN TENNIS PLAYER, ON WHY HE BEAT JIMMY CONNORS AFTER 16 SUCCESSIVE DEFEATS

When the Williams sisters play tennis, it gets pretty hot. When they start grunting, I'm in.

ROBIN WILLIAMS, AMERICAN ACTOR

•••••••••••••••••••••••••••••••

MONICA SELES HAS SO MUCH CONTROL OF THE RACQUET WITH THOSE DOUBLE-HANDED WRISTS.

VIRGINIA WADE, ENGLISH TENNIS PLAYER

•••••••••••••••••••••••••••••••

Federer is just the third person ever to achieve this impossible feat.

BBC RADIO 5 LIVE COMMENTARY

ANN'S GOT TO TAKE HER NERVES BY THE HORN.

VIRGINIA WADE, ENGLISH TENNIS PLAYER

. . . .

Stay in school, kids, or you'll end up being an umpire.

ANDY RODDICK, AMERICAN TENNIS PLAYER

. . . .

STRAWBERRIES, CREAM AND CHAMPERS FLOWED LIKE HOT CAKES.

BBC RADIO 2 COMMENTARY

She puts her head
**DOWN AND
BANGS IT**
STRAIGHT
ACROSS THE LINE.

ANN JONES, ENGLISH TENNIS
PLAYER AND COMMENTATOR

I'd rather be No. 2 in Chile
and No. 1 in the world.

**NICOLÁS MASSÚ ON BEING CHILE'S
TOP TENNIS PLAYER**

• •

BILLIE JEAN KING, WITH THE
LOOK ON HER FACE THAT SAYS
SHE CAN'T BELIEVE IT, BECAUSE
SHE NEVER BELIEVES IT, AND YET,
SOMEHOW, I THINK SHE DOES.

MAX ROBERTSON, BRITISH SPORTS PRESENTER

• •

The pace of this match is really
accelerating, by which I mean it's
getting faster all the time.

DAVID COLEMAN, ENGLISH SPORTS PRESENTER

JOHN McENROE

The American John McEnroe was one of the best tennis players of all time, but was just as famous for being the bad boy of the sport. To everyone's surprise he then metamorphosed into the most genial of tennis commentators, delighting us with amusing quotes – some intended, some not so much.

THAT'S ONE OF THE BEST SETS
I'VE SEEN HIM PLAY, ALTHOUGH I
SHOULD PREFACE THAT BY SAYING
I HAVEN'T SEEN HIM PLAY BEFORE.

....

LET'S HOPE HIS NERVES WILL RUN
THROUGH HIS VEINS.

....

HERE WE SEE ANDRE SA,
WHO, NEVER HAVING WON A
COMPETITIVE MATCH, HAS
REACHED THE WIMBLEDON
QUARTER-FINAL.

IT'S BEEN PREDICTABLE, IN
THE SENSE OF 'EXPECT THE
UNEXPECTED'.

....

TENNIS IS A FUNNY GAME, WITH
UNBELIEVABLE HIGHS, AND THE
LOWS ARE JUST AS LOW.

....

THE OLDER YOU GET, THE BETTER
YOU USED TO BE.

MICHAEL CHANG HAS ALL THE FIRE AND PASSION OF A PUBLIC SERVICE ANNOUNCEMENT – HE MAKES PETE SAMPRAS APPEAR FASCINATING.

ALEX RAMSEY, BRITISH TENNIS WRITER

....

It's cool, overcast and cloudy here – but in a few moments two great players will take the long walk down the tunnel and emerge into the Melbourne sunshine.

JOHN ALEXANDER, AUSTRALIAN TENNIS PLAYER AND COMMENTATOR

....

TIM HENMAN'S INJURED SHOULDER HAS RAISED ITS UGLY HEAD AGAIN.

JONATHAN OVEREND, BBC RADIO 5 LIVE COMMENTATOR

Lleyton Hewitt – his two greatest strengths are his legs, his speed, his agility and his competitiveness.

PAT CASH, AUSTRALIAN TENNIS PLAYER

....

HENMAN AND CORIA HAVE MET THREE TIMES IN THE PAST AND THEY'VE WON ONE APIECE.

ANNABEL CROFT, ENGLISH TENNIS PLAYER

....

Tim Henman, I guess, is sitting in the locker room, pacing up and down.

JOHN INVERDALE, ENGLISH SPORTS PRESENTER

If you're up against a girl with big boobs, bring her to the net, and make her hit backhand volleys. That's the hardest shot for the well endowed.

BILLIE JEAN KING,
AMERICAN TENNIS PLAYER

ANDRE SA IS PLAYING CLOSE TO HIS POTENTIAL – MAYBE EVEN ABOVE IT.

BORIS BECKER, GERMAN TENNIS PLAYER AND COMMENTATOR

• •

He has great pressure on his shoulders internally.

BBC RADIO 5 LIVE COMMENTARY

• •

THE FIRST THING IS, IT'S INEVITABLE. THE SECOND THING IS, IT'S GOING TO HAPPEN ANYWAY.

GERALD WILLIAMS, ENGLISH TENNIS JOURNALIST

To err is human. To put the blame
on someone else is doubles.

ANONYMOUS

. . . .

CHIP HOOPER IS SUCH A BIG MAN
THAT IT IS SOMETIMES DIFFICULT
TO SEE WHERE HE IS ON THE COURT.

MARK COX, ENGLISH TENNIS PLAYER

. . . .

If she gets the jitters now, then she
isn't the great champion that she is.

MAX ROBERTSON, BRITISH SPORTS PRESENTER

ZIVOJINOVIC SEEMS TO BE
ABLE TO PULL THE BIG BULLET
OUT OF THE TOP DRAWER.

MIKE INGHAM, ENGLISH SPORTS COMMENTATOR

· ·

Strangely enough, Kathy Jordan
is getting to the net first,
which she always does.

FRED PERRY, ENGLISH TENNIS PLAYER

· ·

SHE COMES FROM A TENNIS-
PLAYING FAMILY. HER
FATHER'S A DENTIST.

BBC2 TV COMMENTARY

Arantxa Sánchez Vicario is the only sports person whose name is worth 175 in *Scrabble*.

NICK HANCOCK, ENGLISH TV PRESENTER

....

THEY SHOULD SEND BORG AWAY TO ANOTHER PLANET. WE PLAY TENNIS. HE PLAYS SOMETHING ELSE.

ILIE NĂSTASE, ROMANIAN TENNIS PLAYER, ON HIS SWEDISH RIVAL

....

These ball boys are marvellous. You don't even notice them. There's a left-handed one over there. I noticed him earlier.

MAX ROBERTSON, BRITISH SPORTS PRESENTER

DAN MASKELL

'Oh, I say!' and 'Quite extraordinary!' were just two of the catchphrases of Dan Maskell, the BBC's 'voice of Wimbledon' for over 40 years. Some of his tennis commentary was even more celebrated than his famous catchphrases.

AND HERE'S ZIVIJINOVIC, 6 FOOT
6 INCHES TALL AND WEIGHING
14 POUNDS 10 OUNCES.

· ·

THE GULLIKSON TWINS HERE,
AN INTERESTING PAIR, BOTH
FROM WISCONSIN.

· ·

WHEN MARTINA IS TENSE IT
HELPS HER RELAX.

· ·

THERE IS PETER GRAF,
STEFFI'S FATHER, WITH HIS
HEAD ON HIS CHIN.

LENDL HAS REMAINED AS CALM
AS THE PROVERBIAL ICEBERG
THROUGHOUT.

•••••••••••••••••••••••••••••••

HE SLIPS, BUT MANAGES TO
REGROUP HIMSELF.

•••••••••••••••••••••••••••••••

YOU CAN ALMOST HEAR THE
SILENCE AS THEY BATTLE IT OUT.

HORSING
AROUND

A REAL RACEHORSE SHOULD
HAVE A HEAD LIKE A LADY
AND A BEHIND LIKE A COOK.

JACK LEACH, ENGLISH JOCKEY

Horse sense is what keeps horses
from betting on what people will do.

ANONYMOUS

OWNING A RACEHORSE IS
PROBABLY THE MOST EXPENSIVE
WAY OF GETTING ON TO A
RACECOURSE FOR NOTHING.

CLEMENT FREUD, BRITISH WRITER AND BROADCASTER

Riding is the art of keeping a horse between yourself and the ground.

ANONYMOUS

• •

HORSE RACING IS ANIMATED ROULETTE.

ROGER KAHN, AMERICAN WRITER

• •

A bookie is just a pickpocket who lets you use your own hands.

HENRY MORGAN, AMERICAN ACTOR

One way to stop a
runaway horse is
to bet on him.

JEFFREY BERNARD,
ENGLISH JOURNALIST

THERE ARE, THEY SAY, FOOLS, BLOODY FOOLS, AND MEN WHO REMOUNT IN A STEEPLECHASE.

JOHN OAKSEY, ENGLISH HORSE RACING COMMENTATOR

....

Playing polo is like trying to play golf during an earthquake.

SYLVESTER STALLONE, AMERICAN ACTOR

....

THAT REALLY IS A LOVELY HORSE. I ONCE RODE HER MOTHER.

TED WALSH, IRISH JOCKEY AND TRAINER

Money, horse racing and women – three things the boys just can't figure out.

WILL ROGERS, AMERICAN ENTERTAINER

· ·

STEVE CAUTHEN, WELL ON HIS WAY TO THAT MYTHICAL 200 MARK.

JIMMY LINDLEY, ENGLISH JOCKEY AND COMMENTATOR

· ·

In 1900 the owner of the Grand National winner was the then Prince of Wales, King Edward VII.

DAVID COLEMAN, ENGLISH SPORTS PRESENTER

HE'S A VERY COMPETITIVE COMPETITOR. THAT'S THE SORT OF COMPETITOR HE IS.

DORIAN WILLIAMS, ENGLISH SHOW JUMPER AND COMMENTATOR

• •

And the judge has called for a photo, appropriately for the Bonusprint Sirenia Stakes.

GRAHAM GOODE, BRITISH HORSE RACING COMMENTATOR

• •

I HAVE NO INTENTION OF WATCHING UNDERSIZED ENGLISHMEN PERCHED ON HORSES WITH MATCHSTICK LEGS RACE ALONG COURSES PLANNED TO AMUSE NELL GWYNN.

GILBERT HARDING, ENGLISH JOURNALIST

The world should be postponed
for a whore and a horse race.

HORACE WALPOLE, BRITISH NOVELIST AND POLITICIAN

· ·

MY HORSE WAS IN THE LEAD,
COMING DOWN THE HOME
STRETCH, BUT THE CADDIE FELL OFF.

SAMUEL GOLDWYN, AMERICAN FILM PRODUCER

· ·

When I appear in public, people
expect me to neigh, grind my
teeth, paw the ground and swish
my tail – none of which is easy.

**PRINCESS ANNE, BRITISH ROYAL AND
KEEN HORSEWOMAN**

Secretariat and Riva Ridge

ARE THE MOST FAMOUS PAIR OF

STABLEMATES
SINCE JOSEPH
AND MARY.

DICK SCHAAP, AMERICAN SPORTS
WRITER, ON THE TWO KENTUCKY
DERBY WINNERS

IN RACING, TO INSULT A MAN'S HORSE IS WORSE THAN INSULTING HIS WIFE.

JOHN OAKSEY, BRITISH SPORTS COMMENTATOR AND JOCKEY

. . . .

Ascot is so exclusive that it is the only race-course in the world where the horses own the people.

ART BUCHWALD, AMERICAN WRITER

THESE TWO HORSES HAVE MET FIVE TIMES THIS SEASON, AND I THINK THEY'VE BEATEN EACH OTHER ON EACH OCCASION.

JIMMY LINDLEY, ENGLISH JOCKEY AND COMMENTATOR

....

Why all the fuss? After all, the Derby is just another race.

LESTER PIGGOTT, ENGLISH JOCKEY, ON WINNING THE DERBY IN 1954 AT THE AGE OF 18

....

A JUMP JOCKEY HAS TO THROW HIS HEART OVER THE FENCE – AND THEN GO OVER AND CATCH IT.

DICK FRANCIS, BRITISH JOCKEY AND NOVELIST

ON YOUR
BIKE!

Learn to swear in different languages. Other riders will appreciate your efforts to communicate.

ROBERT MILLAR, SCOTTISH CYCLIST

....

IT'S THE ONLY RACE IN THE WORLD WHERE YOU HAVE TO GET A HAIRCUT HALFWAY THROUGH.

CHRIS BOARDMAN, ENGLISH CYCLIST, ON THE TOUR DE FRANCE

....

And you join us at a thrilling point of the Madison – with just 112 laps to go!

BBC COMMENTARY

Training is like fighting with a gorilla. You don't stop when you're tired. You stop when the gorilla is tired.

GREG HENDERSON,
NEW ZEALAND CYCLIST

IF YOU BRAKE, YOU DON'T WIN.

MARIO CIPOLLINI, ITALIAN CYCLIST

....

It never gets easier, you just go faster.

GREG LEMOND, AMERICAN CYCLIST

....

AS LONG AS I BREATHE, I ATTACK.

BERNARD HINAULT, FRENCH CYCLIST

The Tour de France produces in me such **PERSISTENT SATISFACTION THAT MY SALIVA FLOWS IN IMPERCEPTIBLE BUT STUBBORN STREAMS.**

SALVADOR DALÍ, SPANISH PAINTER

Next time you are in a car travelling at
40 mph, think about jumping out – naked.
That's what it's like when we crash.

DAVID MILLAR, SCOTTISH CYCLIST

....

TO PREPARE FOR A RACE, THERE
IS NOTHING BETTER THAN
A GOOD PHEASANT, SOME
CHAMPAGNE AND A WOMAN.

JACQUES ANQUETIL, FRENCH CYCLIST

PHIL LIGGETT

We owe the best lines of the cycling world to revered English cycling commentator Phil Liggett. Here are some classic examples of his surreal observations, known as 'Liggettisms'.

THE PELOTON IS PASSING A FIELD OF WHITE COWS. THIS REGION OF FRANCE IS KNOWN FOR ITS BOVINE... OF COURSE, NONE OF THAT MATTERS TO ANY OF THE RIDERS, EXCEPT THAT THEY MIGHT LIKE A NICE STEAK AT THE END OF THE DAY.

....

HE LOOKS BETWEEN HIS LEGS AND SEES NOBODY THERE!

....

HAVING BEEN ROBBED OF THE DAY'S PRIZE, YOU'LL NOTICE THE BIG SPRINTERS AREN'T AT THE FRONT SHARPENING THEIR LEGS.

WE ARE NOW DEEP INTO THE
INTESTINES OF THE ALPS.

· ·

HE'LL HAVE TO REACH INTO HIS
SUITCASE OF COURAGE!

· ·

A MOST IMMODEST WAY.

· ·

HE'S BEEN THROWN A BONE AND
IT SURE IS A MEATY ONE.

HINCAPIE IS IN FRONT
BREAKING THE WIND.

....

LOOK AT RICCARDO RICCÒ.
WHERE ON THE MOUNTAIN DID HE
BUY A NEW SET OF LEGS?

....

THIS IS A PEDIGREE GROUP OF
MEN. THEY ARE HOLDING ON BY
THE SKIN OF THEIR SHORTS.

....

GREG LEMOND HAS LITERALLY
COME BACK FROM THE DEAD TO
LEAD THE TOUR DE FRANCE.

GETTING INTO THE SWING OF THINGS

Columbus went around the world in 1492. That isn't a lot of strokes when you consider the course.

LEE TREVINO, AMERICAN GOLFER

....

I NEED A DOCTOR. RING THE NEAREST GOLF CLUB.

GROUCHO MARX, AMERICAN COMIC ACTOR

....

The more I practise, the luckier I get.

GARY PLAYER, SOUTH AFRICAN GOLFER

I KNOW I'M GETTING BETTER
AT GOLF BECAUSE I'M HITTING
FEWER SPECTATORS.

GERALD FORD, AMERICAN PRESIDENT

. . . .

Sudden success in golf is like the
sudden acquisition of wealth. It is apt to
unsettle and deteriorate the character.

P. G. WODEHOUSE, ENGLISH WRITER

. . . .

MAN BLAMES FATE FOR ALL OTHER
ACCIDENTS, BUT FEELS PERSONALLY
RESPONSIBLE FOR A HOLE-IN-ONE.

MARTHA BECKMAN, AMERICAN WRITER

Golf is the cruellest of sports.

IT'S A HARLOT, AN OBSESSION,

A BOULEVARD OF BROKEN DREAMS.

JIM MURRAY, ENGLISH WRITER AND JOURNALIST

PETER ALLISS

Ex-professional golfer and popular TV commentator Peter Alliss is well known for sometimes letting his tongue run ahead of his brain. Here are some of the Englishman's finest moments.

THEY'LL BE CHASING KANGAROOS ROUND THE COOLABONG TONIGHT.

AFTER AUSTRALIAN ADAM SCOTT WON THE MASTERS

....

NOT IN THOSE TROUSERS, SIR. NOT AT THIS CLUB. TRY THE MUNICIPAL COURSE.

....

A LITTLE PREMATURE, MY COCK-A-LEEKIE.

AFTER TIGER WOODS MISSED A PUTT ON THE LOW SIDE OF THE HOLE

I HAVEN'T SEEN A GRIP LIKE THAT
SINCE THEY CLOSED THE GENTS AT
KING'S CROSS STATION.

....

IN TECHNICAL TERMS,
HE'S MAKING A REAL PIG'S
EAR OF THIS HOLE.

....

– MID TO LATE FORTIES – WHEN
THINGS START TO HAPPEN TO
THE HUMAN BODY.

....

AS THE COCK CROWS, IT'S ONLY
ABOUT 200 YARDS.

Golf is a game in which you can claim the privileges of age and retain the playthings of childhood.

SAMUEL JOHNSON, ENGLISH WRITER

. . . .

GOLF AND SEX ARE THE ONLY THINGS YOU CAN ENJOY WITHOUT BEING GOOD AT THEM.

ANONYMOUS

. . . .

Golf is so popular simply because it is the best game in the world at which to be bad.

A. A. MILNE, ENGLISH WRITER

MY FAVOURITE SHOTS ARE THE PRACTICE SWING AND THE CONCEDED PUTT. THE REST CAN NEVER BE MASTERED.

GEORGE ROBERTSON, SCOTTISH POLITICIAN

. . . .

Golf is a game that needlessly prolongs the lives of some of our most useless citizens.

BOB HOPE, AMERICAN COMEDIAN AND ACTOR

. . . .

ALL I'VE GOT AGAINST IT IS THAT IT TAKES YOU SO FAR FROM THE CLUBHOUSE.

ERIC LINKLATER, SCOTTISH NOVELIST

The uglier a man's legs are, the better he plays golf. It's almost a law.

H. G. WELLS, ENGLISH WRITER

• •

NEVER TRY TO KEEP MORE THAN 300 SEPARATE THOUGHTS IN YOUR MIND DURING YOUR SWING.

HENRY BEARD, AMERICAN HUMORIST

• •

I'm learning not to get too excited after one good round and to keep my head on the ground.

COLIN MONTGOMERIE, SCOTTISH GOLFER

I WOULD LIKE TO THANK
MY PARENTS, ESPECIALLY MY
FATHER AND MOTHER.

**GREG NORMAN, AUSTRALIAN GOLFER
(DURING A WINNER'S SPEECH)**

· ·

So, Woosie, you're from Wales.
What part of Scotland is that?

**AMERICAN JOURNALIST TO WELSH
GOLFER IAN WOOSNAM**

· ·

TO SAY I WAS DISAPPOINTED
WOULD BE LIKE SAYING CUSTER
HAD A SPOT OF BOTHER
AT LITTLE BIGHORN.

**TONY JACKLIN, ENGLISH GOLFER
(AFTER A POOR ROUND)**

Arnie would go for the flag from the middle of an alligator's back.

LEE TREVINO,
AMERICAN
GOLFER, ON
ARNOLD
PALMER

Although golf was originally restricted to wealthy Protestants, today it's open to anybody who owns hideous clothing.

DAVE BARRY, AMERICAN AUTHOR AND COLUMNIST

· ·

GIVE ME A MAN WITH BIG HANDS AND BIG FEET AND NO BRAINS AND I'LL MAKE A GOLFER OUT OF HIM.

WALTER HAGEN, AMERICAN GOLFER

· ·

Most new sets of golf clubs still include three-irons, even though most regular golfers would get more use from a second umbrella.

DAVID OWEN, AMERICAN GOLF WRITER

MUIRFIELD WITHOUT A WIND
IS LIKE A LADY UNDRESSED.
NO CHALLENGE.

**TOM WATSON, AMERICAN GOLFER, ON
THE SCOTTISH GOLF COURSE**

....

Husband: I got a new set
of clubs for my wife.
Friend: That sounds like a fair swap.

BILL WANNAN, AUSTRALIAN HUMORIST

....

I WAS SWINGING LIKE A TOILET
DOOR ON A PRAWN TRAWLER.

DAVID FEHERTY, NORTHERN IRISH GOLFER

THE NEED
FOR SPEED

If everything seems under control,
you're just not going fast enough.

MARIO ANDRETTI, ITALIAN-AMERICAN RACING DRIVER

· ·

YOU WIN SOME, YOU LOSE
SOME, YOU WRECK SOME.

DALE EARNHARDT, AMERICAN RACING DRIVER

· ·

Calling upon my years of experience,
I froze at the controls.

STIRLING MOSS, ENGLISH RACING DRIVER

Grand Prix driving is like balancing an egg on a spoon while shooting the rapids.

GRAHAM HILL,
ENGLISH RACING DRIVER

EVERY CAR HAS A LOT OF SPEED
IN IT. THE TRICK IS GETTING
THE SPEED OUT OF IT.

A. J. FOY, AMERICAN RACING DRIVER

Some of the ravines are so deep that if
you topple over, your clothes will be out
of date by the time you hit the bottom.

**TONY POND, ENGLISH RALLY DRIVER, ON THE
DANGERS OF THE MONTE CARLO RALLY**

YOU DRIVE THE CAR;
YOU DON'T CARRY IT.

**JANET GUTHRIE, AMERICAN RACING DRIVER,
ON BEING ASKED IF FEMALE DRIVERS WERE AS
STRONG AS THEIR MALE COUNTERPARTS**

MURRAY WALKER

English motorsport commentator Murray Walker
was the voice of motor racing for decades.
His enthusiasm knew no bounds and he often
became overexcited about what he was seeing
unfold before him, leading to some priceless
commentary. Here are some of his
greatest moments.

THIS HAS BEEN A GREAT SEASON
FOR NELSON PIQUET, AS HE IS NOW
KNOWN, AND ALWAYS HAS BEEN.

....

AND MARK BLUNDELL HAS
STOPPED WITH HIS FRONT
WHEELS STATIONARY.

....

IF IS A BIG WORD IN FORMULA 1.
IN FACT, IF IS FORMULA 1
BACKWARDS.

....

THAT'S HISTORY. I SAY HISTORY
BECAUSE IT HAPPENED IN
THE PAST.

YOU MIGHT THINK THAT'S
NOT CRICKET, AND IT'S NOT.
IT'S MOTOR RACING.

....

MANSELL CAN SEE HIM
IN HIS EARPHONE.

....

HE'S OBVIOUSLY GONE IN FOR
A PIT STOP. I SAY OBVIOUSLY,
BECAUSE I CAN'T SEE A THING.

....

ONLY A FEW MORE LAPS TO GO
AND THEN THE ACTION WILL
BEGIN. UNLESS THIS IS THE
ACTION, WHICH IT IS!

IT'S LAP 26 OF 58, WHICH UNLESS I'M VERY MUCH MISTAKEN IS HALFWAY.

....

MANSELL IS SLOWING DOWN, TAKING IT EASY. OH NO, HE ISN'T – IT'S A LAP RECORD!

....

PATRICK TAMBAY'S HOPES, WHICH WERE NIL BEFORE, ARE ABSOLUTELY ZERO NOW.

....

NOW HE MUST NOT GO THE WRONG WAY ROUND THE CIRCUIT, AND UNLESS HE CAN SPIN HIMSELF STATIONARY THROUGH 360 DEGREES I FAIL TO SEE HOW HE CAN AVOID DOING SO.

THERE ARE SEVEN WINNERS OF THE MONACO GRAND PRIX ON THE STARTING LINE TODAY, AND FOUR OF THEM ARE MICHAEL SCHUMACHER.

....

THE LEADING CAR IS ABSOLUTELY UNIQUE, EXCEPT FOR THE ONE BEHIND IT, WHICH IS ABSOLUTELY IDENTICAL.

....

DO MY EYES DECEIVE ME, OR IS SENNA'S LOTUS SOUNDING ROUGH?

....

EXCUSE ME WHILE I INTERRUPT MYSELF.

THIS IS AN INTERESTING CIRCUIT, BECAUSE IT HAS INCLINES. AND NOT JUST UP, BUT DOWN AS WELL.

....

NIGEL MANSELL IS THE LAST PERSON IN THE RACE APART FROM THE FIVE IN FRONT OF HIM.

....

BRUNDLE IS DRIVING AN ABSOLUTELY PLUPERFECT RACE.

....

THERE'S NOTHING WRONG WITH HIS CAR EXCEPT THAT IT'S ON FIRE.

THACKWELL REALLY
CAN METAPHORICALLY
COAST HOME NOW.

....

I KNOW IT'S AN OLD CLICHÉ, BUT
YOU CAN CUT THE ATMOSPHERE
WITH A CRICKET STUMP.

....

HOW YOU CAN CRASH INTO A
WALL WITHOUT IT BEING THERE IN
THE FIRST PLACE IS BEYOND ME.

....

UNLESS I AM VERY MUCH
MISTAKEN… I AM VERY
MUCH MISTAKEN!

There are two things no man will admit he can't do well: drive and make love.

STIRLING MOSS, ENGLISH RACING DRIVER

....

RACING IS 99 PER CENT BOREDOM, 1 PER CENT TERROR.

GEOFF BRABHAM, AUSTRALIAN RACING DRIVER

....

I'm a full-blooded racer. What do people think we are here for, a Sunday outing?

MICHAEL SCHUMACHER, GERMAN RACING DRIVER

The drivers have
one foot on the

BRAKE, ONE ON
THE CLUTCH

AND ONE ON
THE THROTTLE.

BOB VARSHA, AMERICAN
MOTORSPORT ANNOUNCER

AERODYNAMICS ARE FOR PEOPLE WHO CAN'T BUILD ENGINES.

ENZO FERRARI, ITALIAN MOTOR RACER AND ENTREPRENEUR

....

Winning is everything. The only ones who remember you when you come second are your wife and your dog.

DAMON HILL, ENGLISH RACING DRIVER

....

TO FINISH FIRST, YOU MUST FIRST FINISH.

JUAN MANUEL FANGIO, ARGENTINE RACING DRIVER

THE
BEAUTIFUL
GAME

We had a good team on paper.
Unfortunately, the game
was played on grass.

BRIAN CLOUGH, ENGLISH FOOTBALL MANAGER

. . . .

THE FAT LADY HASN'T STARTED TO SING YET, BUT SHE HAS A MIC IN HER HAND.

IAN HOLLOWAY, ENGLISH FOOTBALL MANAGER, ON HIS TEAM'S CHANCES OF AVOIDING RELEGATION

. . . .

I can play in the centre, on the right
and occasionally on the left side.

DAVID BECKHAM, ENGLISH FOOTBALLER, ON BEING ASKED WHETHER HE CONSIDERED HIMSELF TO BE A VOLATILE PLAYER

ALLY MACLEOD THINKS THAT TACTICS ARE A NEW KIND OF MINT.

BILLY CONNOLLY, SCOTTISH COMEDIAN, ON THE THEN SCOTLAND FOOTBALL MANAGER

• •

That's great, tell him he's Pelé and get him back on.

JOHN LAMBIE, SCOTTISH FOOTBALL MANAGER, ON BEING TOLD THAT A CONCUSSED STRIKER DID NOT KNOW WHO HE WAS

• •

SOME YOU LOSE, SOME YOU DRAW.

JASPER CARROTT, ENGLISH COMEDIAN, ON BEING A BIRMINGHAM CITY SUPPORTER

No, I'm just going to crumble like a wreck. I'll go home, become an alcoholic and maybe jump off a bridge.

GORDON STRACHAN, SCOTTISH FOOTBALLER AND MANAGER, ON BEING ASKED WHETHER HE COULD COPE WITH THE END OF HIS TEAM'S WINNING RUN

. . . .

YOU'RE NOT A REAL MANAGER UNTIL YOU'VE BEEN SACKED.

MALCOLM ALLISON, ENGLISH FOOTBALL MANAGER

You have to be a masochist to
be an international manager.

ARSÈNE WENGER, FRENCH FOOTBALL MANAGER

. . . .

AN OXYMORON IS WHEN TWO
CONTRADICTORY CONCEPTS
ARE JUXTAPOSED, AS IN
'FOOTBALLING BRAIN'.

PATRICK MURRAY, ENGLISH ACTOR

. . . .

We're a young side that
will only get younger.

PAUL HART, ENGLISH FOOTBALL MANAGER

Ian Rush unleashed his left foot and it hit the back of the net.

MIKE ENGLAND,
WELSH FOOTBALLER
AND MANAGER

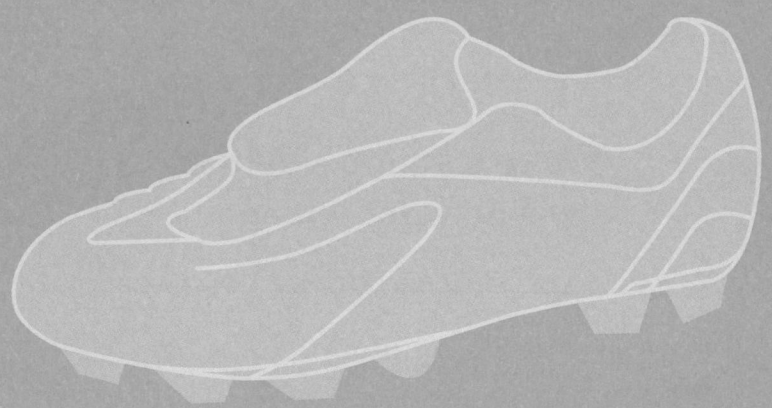

THE MATCH WILL BE SHOWN ON
MATCH OF THE DAY THIS EVENING.
IF YOU DON'T WANT TO KNOW
THE RESULT, LOOK AWAY NOW
AS WE SHOW YOU TONY ADAMS
LIFTING THE TROPHY FOR ARSENAL.

STEVE RIDER, ENGLISH SPORTS PRESENTER

· ·

If the fourth official had done his
job it wouldn't have happened, but
I don't want to blame anyone.

JOHN ALDRIDGE, IRISH FOOTBALLER AND MANAGER

BOBBY ROBSON'S NATURAL
EXPRESSION IS THAT OF A
MAN WHO FEARS HE MIGHT
HAVE LEFT THE GAS ON.

DAVID LACEY, ENGLISH SPORTS JOURNALIST

....

My parents have been there for me
ever since I was about seven.

DAVID BECKHAM, ENGLISH FOOTBALLER

....

THERE'S NO WAY RYAN GIGGS
IS ANOTHER GEORGE BEST. HE'S
ANOTHER RYAN GIGGS.

DENIS LAW, SCOTTISH FOOTBALLER

When it comes to the David Beckhams of the world, this guy's up there with Roberto Carlos.

DUNCAN McKENZIE, ENGLISH FOOTBALLER

· ·

ANYONE WHO USES THE WORD 'QUINTESSENTIALLY' IN A HALF-TIME TEAM TALK IS TALKING CRAP.

MICK McCARTHY, IRISH FOOTBALL MANAGER

· ·

He's had two cruciates and a broken ankle. That's not easy. Every player attached to the club is praying the boy gets a break.

ALEX FERGUSON, SCOTTISH FOOTBALL MANAGER, ON WES BROWN

AS A SMALL BOY I WAS TORN
BETWEEN TWO AMBITIONS: TO BE
A FOOTBALLER OR TO RUN AWAY
AND JOIN A CIRCUS. AT PARTICK
THISTLE I GOT TO DO BOTH.

ALAN HANSEN, SCOTTISH FOOTBALLER AND PUNDIT

. . . .

I spent a lot of money on booze, birds
and fast cars. The rest I just squandered.

GEORGE BEST, NORTHERN IRISH FOOTBALLER

. . . .

AND ZIDANE WILL BE GIVEN
A PRIVATE POOL, WITH A
GARDENER THROWN IN.

DES CAHILL, IRISH SPORTS PRESENTER

What I said to them at half-time
wouldn't be printable on the radio.

GERRY FRANCIS, ENGLISH FOOTBALLER AND MANAGER

• •

THE GROIN'S A LITTLE SORE BUT
AFTER THE SEMI–FINAL I PUT IT
TO THE BACK OF MY HEAD.

MICHAEL HUGHES, NORTHERN IRISH FOOTBALLER

• •

It was a match that could have gone
either way and very nearly did.

JIM SHERWIN, IRISH SPORTS COMMENTATOR

ACHILLES TENDONS ARE A PAIN IN THE BUTT.

DAVID O'LEARY, IRISH FOOTBALLER AND MANAGER

• •

I don't think we'll go down. But then again, the captain of the Titanic said the same thing.

NEVILLE SOUTHALL, WELSH FOOTBALLER, ON EVERTON'S CHANCES OF AVOIDING RELEGATION

• •

THE SECRET OF FOOTBALL IS TO EQUALISE BEFORE THE OPPOSITION SCORES.

DANNY BLANCHFLOWER, NORTHERN IRISH FOOTBALLER AND MANAGER

If Everton were playing down
at the bottom of my garden,
I'd draw the curtains.

BILL SHANKLY, SCOTTISH FOOTBALL MANAGER

....

WINNING ISN'T THE END
OF THE WORLD.

DAVID PLEAT, ENGLISH FOOTBALL MANAGER

....

Liam Brady's been playing inside
Platini's shorts all night.

JIMMY MAGEE, IRISH SPORTS BROADCASTER

VELOCITY.

KENNY DALGLISH, SCOTTISH FOOTBALLER AND MANAGER, AS HE DASHED BY A REPORTER ASKING HIM FOR 'A QUICK WORD'

• •

Most players would give their right arm for his left foot.

MARK LAWRENSON, IRISH FOOTBALLER AND PUNDIT, ON JASON WILCOX

• •

I WONDER WHAT WOULD HAVE HAPPENED IF THE SHIRT HAD BEEN ON THE OTHER FOOT.

MIKE WALKER, WELSH FOOTBALLER AND MANAGER

My best moment? I have a lot of
good moments, but the one I prefer
is when I kicked the hooligan.

ERIC CANTONA, FRENCH FOOTBALLER

· ·

AND KEEGAN WAS THERE LIKE
A SURGEON'S KNIFE – BANG!

BYRON BUTLER, ENGLISH FOOTBALL WRITER

· ·

The walking wounded are
starting to walk.

**PHIL BROWN, ENGLISH FOOTBALL MANAGER,
ON HIS TEAM'S INJURY LIST**

Look, if you're in the penalty area and aren't quite sure

WHAT TO DO WITH THE BALL, JUST STICK IT IN THE NET

AND WE'LL DISCUSS ALL YOUR OPTIONS AFTERWARDS.

BOB PAISLEY, ENGLISH
FOOTBALL MANAGER

PAUL SCHOLES IS A FANTASTIC
MIDFIELDER. THERE'S NOT A
WEAKNESS THAT HE HASN'T GOT.

STEVE BRUCE, ENGLISH FOOTBALLER AND MANAGER

· ·

The boys' feet have been up in
the clouds since the win.

ALAN BUCKLEY, ENGLISH FOOTBALLER AND MANAGER

· ·

THE BEAUTY OF CUP FOOTBALL
IS THAT JACK ALWAYS HAS A
CHANCE OF BEATING GOLIATH.

**TERRY BUTCHER, ENGLISH FOOTBALLER
AND MANAGER**

Butcher goes forward as Ipswich throw their last trump card into the fire.

BYRON BUTLER, ENGLISH FOOTBALL WRITER AND COMMENTATOR

....

THERE ARE TWO GREAT TEAMS ON MERSEYSIDE: LIVERPOOL AND LIVERPOOL RESERVES.

BILL SHANKLY, SCOTTISH FOOTBALL MANAGER

....

What a goal! One for the Puritans.

CAPITAL GOLD RADIO COMMENTATOR

IN 1969 I GAVE UP WOMEN AND
ALCOHOL – IT WAS THE WORST
20 MINUTES OF MY LIFE.

GEORGE BEST, NORTHERN IRISH FOOTBALLER

· ·

I have to sit down with him
and see where we stand.

**ARSÈNE WENGER, FRENCH FOOTBALL MANAGER,
ON PATRICK VIEIRA**

· ·

THE PROBLEMS AT WIMBLEDON
SEEM TO BE THAT THE CLUB HAS
SUFFERED A LOSS OF COMPLACENCY.

JOE KINNEAR, IRISH FOOTBALLER AND MANAGER

THE OVAL
GAME

You've got to get your first tackle
in early, even if it's late.

RAY GRAVELL, WELSH RUGBY PLAYER

• •

WE'LL PROBABLY DRINK AS HARD AS WE TRAIN – THAT'S VERY HARD.

STUART BARNES, ENGLISH RUGBY PLAYER AND COMMENTATOR

• •

Rugby league is much, much more
physical than rugby union, and that's
before anyone starts breaking the rules.

ADRIAN HADLEY, WELSH RUGBY PLAYER

NOT MANY PEOPLE IN BATLEY SPEAK LATIN, SO THE FIRST THING WE DID WAS CHANGE THE MOTTO.

STEPHEN BALL ON TAKING OVER AS CHAIRMAN OF THE RUGBY LEAGUE CLUB

· ·

It went well. There are no problems, and, as a bonus, it showed that I have a brain!

CORNÉ KRIGE, SOUTH AFRICAN RUGBY PLAYER, AFTER GOING FOR A BRAIN SCAN

· ·

REFEREES ARE ONLY HUMAN, I THINK.

PHIL KEARNS, AUSTRALIAN RUGBY PLAYER

Rugby is a good occasion for keeping 30 bullies far from the centre of the city.

OSCAR WILDE, IRISH WRITER

· ·

WE'VE LOST SEVEN OF OUR LAST EIGHT MATCHES. THE ONLY TEAM THAT WE'VE BEATEN IS WESTERN SAMOA. GOOD JOB WE DIDN'T PLAY THE WHOLE OF SAMOA.

GARETH DAVIES, WELSH RUGBY PLAYER

· ·

In south-west Lancashire, babes don't toddle, they side-step. Queuing women talk of 'nipping round the blindside'. Rugby league provides our cultural adrenalin.

COLIN WELLAND, ENGLISH SCREENWRITER

Grandmother

OR TAILS, SIR?

REFEREE TO PRINCESS ANNE'S SON
PETER PHILLIPS, ON HIS PRE-
MATCH COIN-TOSS PREFERENCE

I THOUGHT I WOULD HAVE A QUIET PINT – AND ABOUT 17 NOISY ONES.

GARETH CHILCOTT, ENGLISH RUGBY PLAYER, AFTER PLAYING HIS LAST GAME FOR BATH

....

I think you enjoy the game more if you don't know the rules. Anyway, you're at least on the same wavelength as the referees.

JONATHAN DAVIES, WELSH RUGBY PLAYER

....

WHAT A GREAT-SOUNDING NAME. HE SOUNDS LIKE A DRUG DEALER FROM BRAZIL.

MURRAY MEXTED, NEW ZEALAND RUGBY PLAYER AND COMMENTATOR, ON FELLOW KIWI PLAYER RICO GEAR

Just watch the pace of the French defence. They are attacking the Irish defensively.

DAVID FORDHAM, AUSTRALIAN COMMENTATOR

....

I'VE NEVER HAD MAJOR KNEE SURGERY ON ANY OTHER PART OF MY BODY.

JERRY COLLINS, NEW ZEALAND RUGBY PLAYER

....

He scored that try after only 22 seconds, totally against the run of play.

MURRAY MEXTED, NEW ZEALAND RUGBY PLAYER AND COMMENTATOR

ME? AS ENGLAND'S ANSWER
TO JONAH LOMU? JOANNA
LUMLEY, MORE LIKELY.

DAMIAN HOPLEY, ENGLISH RUGBY PLAYER

. . . .

Rugby is a wonderful show. Dance, opera
and, suddenly, the blood of a killing.

RICHARD BURTON, WELSH ACTOR

. . . .

THE IRISH TREAT YOU LIKE
ROYALTY BEFORE AND AFTER
THE GAME, AND KICK YOU
TO PIECES DURING IT.

JEFF PROBYN, ENGLISH RUGBY PLAYER

The French are predictably unpredictable.

ANDREW MEHRTENS, NEW ZEALAND RUGBY PLAYER, AFTER AN ALL BLACKS SURPRISE LOSS TO THE FRENCH IN THE 1999 RUGBY WORLD CUP

• •

RUGBY PLAYERS ARE LIKE LAVA LAMPS: GOOD TO LOOK AT BUT NOT VERY BRIGHT.

ANONYMOUS

• •

We actually got the winning try three minutes from the end but then they scored.

PHIL WAUGH, AUSTRALIAN RUGBY PLAYER

I'M PLEASED TO SAY I DON'T THINK ABOUT RUGBY ALL THE TIME: JUST MOST OF THE TIME.

LAWRENCE DALLAGLIO, ENGLISH RUGBY PLAYER

....

The first half will be even. The second half will be even harder.

TERRY HOLMES, WELSH RUGBY PLAYER

....

HE MOVES WITH THE ELEGANCE OF A COW ON A BICYCLE.

FRANK HYDE, AUSTRALIAN RUGBY PLAYER AND COMMENTATOR, TALKING ABOUT NOEL KELLY

A good defender should be so mean that if he owned the Atlantic Ocean he still wouldn't give you a wave.

MORNE DU PLESSIS,
SOUTH AFRICAN RUGBY PLAYER

I looked at Colin Meads and I saw a great big sheep farmer who carried the ball as if it was an orange pip.

BILL McLAREN, SCOTTISH RUGBY COMMENTATOR

• •

AND THERE WE SEE THE SAD SIGHT OF MARTIN OFFIAH LIMPING OFF WITH A BROKEN FINGER.

RAY FRENCH, ENGLISH RUGBY PLAYER AND COMMENTATOR

• •

In slow-motion replay the ball seemed to hang in the air for even longer.

DAVID ACFIELD, RUGBY COMMENTATOR, ON JONNY WILKINSON'S 2003 WORLD-CUP-WINNING DROP GOAL

BEING DROPPED AND TAKE THAT SPLITTING UP ON THE SAME DAY IS ENOUGH TO FINISH ANYONE OFF.

MARTIN BAYFIELD, ENGLISH RUGBY PLAYER

....

Modern rugby players like to get their retaliation in first.

KIM FLETCHER, AUSTRALIAN SPORTS WRITER

....

YOU NEED A MENTAL TOUGHNESS AND PROBABLY DON'T NEED TO BE TOO BRIGHT.

MARK REGAN, ENGLISH RUGBY PLAYER, ON PLAYING IN THE FRONT ROW

GETTING INTO DEEP WATER

The swimmers are swimming
out of their socks.

**SHARRON DAVIES, ENGLISH SWIMMER
AND COMMENTATOR**

••••••••••••••••••••••••••••••

IF ONE SYNCHRONISED SWIMMER DROWNS, DO THE REST HAVE TO DROWN TOO?

STEVEN WRIGHT, AMERICAN COMEDIAN

••••••••••••••••••••••••••••••

If it had been the backstroke,
I obviously would have stopped.

**MATT ZELEN, AMERICAN SWIMMER, WHOSE TRUNKS
SLIPPED OFF DURING THE BUTTERFLY**

WATER POLO IS TERRIBLY
DANGEROUS. I HAD TWO
HORSES DROWN UNDER ME.

TONY CURTIS, AMERICAN ACTOR

....

This boy swims like a greyhound.

ATHOLE STILL, ENGLISH SPORTS AGENT

....

SWIMMING IS A CONFUSING
SPORT, BECAUSE SOMETIMES YOU
DO IT FOR FUN, AND OTHER
TIMES YOU DO IT NOT TO DIE.

DEMETRI MARTIN, AMERICAN COMEDIAN

If swimming is so good for your figure, how do you explain whales?

STEVEN WRIGHT,
AMERICAN COMEDIAN

It's obvious these Russian swimmers are determined to do well on American soil.

ANITA LONSBOROUGH, ENGLISH SWIMMER

. . . .

WE ARE HOPING THAT OUR SWIMMERS ARE GOING TO DO SOMETHING BIG IN THE POOL.

DIANE MODAHL, ENGLISH ATHLETE

. . . .

I don't see myself competing again. I don't think it will happen. I won't rule it out. I never rule anything out, but it won't happen.

IAN THORPE, AUSTRALIAN SWIMMER

MARIE SCOTT, FROM FLEETWOOD, THE 17-YEAR-OLD WHO HAS REALLY PLUMMETED TO THE TOP.

ALAN WEEKS, ENGLISH SPORTS COMMENTATOR

· ·

I didn't rescue the nation from the depths of Napoleon Bonaparte, but you do the best you can do in your style of racing.

BEN AINSLIE, ENGLISH SAILOR, AFTER WINNING HIS FOURTH OLYMPIC GOLD IN 2012

· ·

AND SHE IS ON THE SHOULDER OF THE HUNGARIAN SWIMMER WHO IS TWO LANES AWAY.

BOB BALLARD, ENGLISH SPORTS PRESENTER

You don't have to

BE LOVERS TO WORK WELL

DAN TOPOLSKI, BRITISH ROWER AND COMMENTATOR, ON BRITISH ROWERS STEVE REDGRAVE AND ANDY HOLMES

It's a good idea to begin at the bottom in everything except in learning to swim.

ANONYMOUS

. . . .

AND, SOMEWHAT SURPRISINGLY, CAMBRIDGE HAVE WON THE TOSS.

HARRY CARPENTER, ENGLISH SPORTS PRESENTER,
ON THE UNIVERSITY BOAT RACE

. . . .

If our swimmers want to win any more medals they'll have to get their skates on.

DAVE BRENNER, BBC SPORTS EDITOR

ROWING IS THE ONLY SPORT THAT ORIGINATED AS A FORM OF CAPITAL PUNISHMENT.

ANONYMOUS

. . . .

I am not particularly talented.

KRISTIN OTTO, GERMAN SWIMMER, WINNER OF SIX OLYMPIC GOLD MEDALS

. . . .

IT'S THE IRON IN THE MIND, NOT IN THE SUPPLEMENTS, THAT WINS MEDALS.

STEVE REDGRAVE, ENGLISH ROWER

THE WINTER SPORTS OF OUR DISCONTENT

The problem with winter sports is that – follow me closely here – they generally take place in winter.

DAVE BARRY, AMERICAN AUTHOR AND COLUMNIST

· ·

CROSS-COUNTRY SKIING IS GREAT IF YOU LIVE IN A SMALL COUNTRY.

STEVEN WRIGHT, AMERICAN COMEDIAN

· ·

The only difference between this and Custer's last stand is that Custer didn't have to look at the tape afterwards.

TERRY CRISP, CANADIAN ICE HOCKEY PLAYER AND COACH (AFTER HIS TEAM LOST 10-0)

All things are

POSSIBLE, EXCEPT FOR SKIING

THROUGH A REVOLVING DOOR.

ANONYMOUS

I DO NOT PARTICIPATE IN ANY SPORT WITH AMBULANCES AT THE BOTTOM OF THE HILL.

ERMA BOMBECK, AMERICAN HUMORIST

. . . .

This is a sport where you can talk about sequins, earrings and plunging necklines – and you are talking about the men.

CHRISTINE BRENNAN, AMERICAN SPORTS COLUMNIST, ON ICE SKATING

. . . .

ICE HOCKEY IS A FORM OF DISORDERLY CONDUCT IN WHICH THE SCORE IS KEPT.

DOUG LARSON, AMERICAN COLUMNIST

Skiing: the art of catching cold and going broke while rapidly heading nowhere at great personal risk.

ANONYMOUS

• •

A PUCK IS A HARD RUBBER DISC THAT HOCKEY PLAYERS STRIKE WHEN THEY CAN'T HIT ONE ANOTHER.

JIMMY CANNON, AMERICAN SPORTS JOURNALIST

• •

Imagine being on a roller coaster, except with your chin just above the track.

SHELLEY RUDMAN, ENGLISH SKELETON BOBSLEDDER, ON HER SPORT

A GOOD HOCKEY PLAYER PLAYS WHERE THE PUCK IS. A GREAT HOCKEY PLAYER PLAYS WHERE THE PUCK IS GOING TO BE.

WAYNE GRETZKY, CANADIAN ICE HOCKEY PLAYER AND COACH

....

Stretch pants – the garment that made skiing a spectator sport.

TIME MAGAZINE

....

HOCKEY PLAYERS WEAR NUMBERS BECAUSE YOU CAN'T ALWAYS IDENTIFY THE BODY WITH DENTAL RECORDS.

BOB PLAGER, CANADIAN ICE HOCKEY PLAYER

Four out of five dentists recommend playing ice hockey.

ANONYMOUS

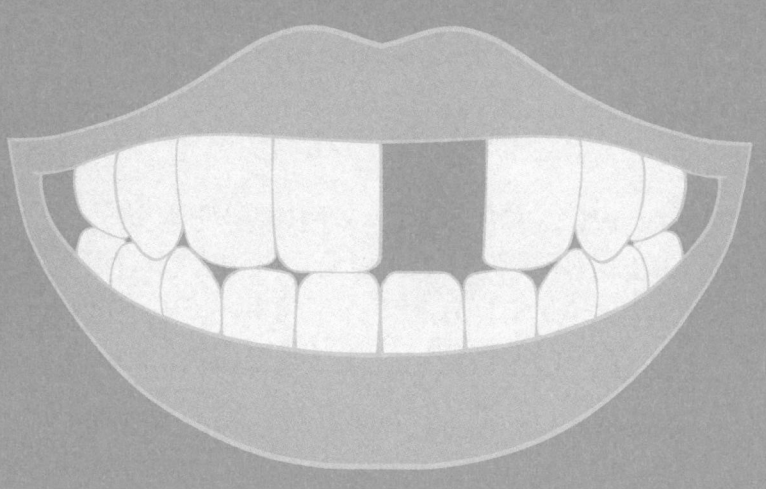

Skiing is the only sport where you spend an arm and a leg to break an arm and a leg.

ANONYMOUS

· ·

OLYMPIC FIGURE SKATING – A SPORT WHERE COMPETITORS ARE DRESSED AS DINNER MINTS.

JERE LONGMAN, AMERICAN SPORTS JOURNALIST

· ·

Skiing combines outdoor fun with knocking down trees with your face.

DAVE BARRY, AMERICAN AUTHOR AND COLUMNIST

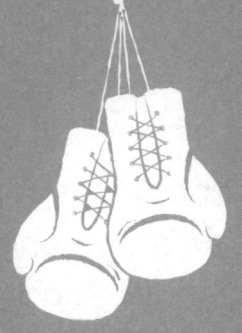

BOXING'S GREATEST HITS

YOU'VE GOT TO REMEMBER THAT GUY'S BASICALLY UNDEFEATED, EXCEPT FOR THAT ONE LOSS.

LENNOX LEWIS, BRITISH–CANADIAN BOXER, ON JOE CALZAGHE

••••••••••••••••••••••••••••••••

If Larry Holmes is the people's champion, then asparagus is the people's vegetable.

BERNIE LINCICOME, AMERICAN SPORTS WRITER

••••••••••••••••••••••••••••••••

I'M ONLY A PRAWN IN THE GAME.

BRIAN LONDON, ENGLISH BOXER

They say that money talks, but the only thing it ever said to me was goodbye.

JOE LOUIS, AMERICAN BOXER

....

IT'S JUST A JOB. GRASS GROWS, BIRDS FLY, WAVES POUND THE SAND. I JUST BEAT PEOPLE UP.

MUHAMMAD ALI, AMERICAN BOXER

....

I miss things like the camaraderie in the gym. I don't miss being smacked in the mouth every day.

BARRY McGUIGAN, BRITISH-IRISH BOXER

BOXING IS A LITTLE LIKE JAZZ. THE BETTER IT IS, THE FEWER PEOPLE CAN UNDERSTAND IT.

GEORGE FOREMAN, AMERICAN BOXER

. . . .

The chances of a rematch for Lennox Lewis are slim and none. And slim is out of town.

DON KING, AMERICAN BOXING PROMOTER

. . . .

ONCE IN THE RING, IT DOESN'T MATTER HOW MANY PEOPLE ARE WATCHING. THEY WON'T BE ABLE TO HELP.

TERRY MARSH, ENGLISH BOXER

I don't mind the title fight going out at three in the morning. Everyone in Glasgow fights at three in the morning.

JIM WATT, SCOTTISH BOXER

. . . .

I WAS CALLED 'REMBRANDT' HOPE IN MY BOXING DAYS, BECAUSE I SPENT SO MUCH TIME ON THE CANVAS.

BOB HOPE, AMERICAN COMEDIAN

. . . .

Sure there have been some deaths and injuries in boxing, but none of them serious.

ALAN MINTER, ENGLISH BOXER

In his prime, Joe Bugner had the physique of a Greek statue, but he had fewer moves.

HUGH McILVANNEY,
SPORTS JOURNALIST

SLEEP CAME, AS IT MUST COME
TO ALL BRITISH HEAVYWEIGHTS,
MIDWAY IN THE FIFTH ROUND.

RED SMITH, AMERICAN SPORTS WRITER

· ·

Don't make me laugh! It's the WBF
belt – I heard they're giving them away
with 5 litres of petrol down at Texaco.

**HERBIE HIDE, BRITISH BOXER, ON AUDLEY HARRISON
WINNING THE WBF HEAVYWEIGHT TITLE**

· ·

TO ME, BOXING IS LIKE A BALLET,
EXCEPT THERE'S NO MUSIC, NO
CHOREOGRAPHY, AND THE
DANCERS HIT EACH OTHER.

JACK HANDEY, AMERICAN HUMORIST

He's a guy who gets up at six o'clock in the morning, regardless of what time it is.

LOU DUVA, AMERICAN BOXING TRAINER

· ·

THERE'S GOING TO BE A REAL DING-DONG WHEN THE BELL GOES.

DAVID COLEMAN, ENGLISH SPORTS COMMENTATOR

· ·

When Bob Arum pats you on the back, he's just looking for a spot to stick the knife.

CUS D'AMATO, AMERICAN BOXING TRAINER

BOXING IS THE ONLY RACKET WHERE YOU'RE ALMOST GUARANTEED TO END UP AS A BUM.

ROCKY GRAZIANO, AMERICAN BOXER

· ·

His new trainer has altered his diet so that they can at least get him to put in his gumshield without coating it in batter.

HARRY PEARSON, ENGLISH SPORTS JOURNALIST, ON BOXER RICKY HATTON

· ·

I'VE SEEN GEORGE FOREMAN SHADOW BOXING AND THE SHADOW WON.

MUHAMMAD ALI, AMERICAN BOXER

If it's undisputed, what's all
the fighting about?

GEORGE CARLIN, AMERICAN COMEDIAN

. . . .

HIS GLOVES. I'VE NEVER BEEN
HIT BY AN EYE IN MY LIFE.

**TERRY DOWNES, ENGLISH BOXER, ON BEING ASKED IF
HE WATCHED HIS OPPONENT'S EYES OR GLOVES**

. . . .

I can only see it going one way,
that's my way. How it's actually
going to go, I can't really say.

NICK WILSHIRE, ENGLISH BOXER

I WANT TO KEEP FIGHTING BECAUSE IT IS THE ONLY THING THAT KEEPS ME OUT OF HAMBURGER JOINTS. IF I DON'T FIGHT, I'LL EAT THE PLANET.

GEORGE FOREMAN, AMERICAN BOXER

You can sum up this sport in two words: you never know.

LOU DUVA, AMERICAN BOXING TRAINER

HIS LEGS TURNED TO SPAGHETTI AND I WAS ALL OVER HIM LIKE THE SAUCE.

VINNIE PAZIENZA, AMERICAN BOXER

HARRY CARPENTER

'Know what I mean, Harry?' became English boxer Frank Bruno's catchphrase, but Harry Carpenter was loved and respected by the boxing fraternity as a whole and by the millions of fans who enjoyed his rich commentary. Here are some of his classic quotes.

HE LOOKS UP AT HIM THROUGH
BLOOD-SMEARED LIPS.

....

THIS BOXER IS DOING WHAT'S
EXPECTED OF HIM, BLEEDING
FROM THE NOSE.

....

PEDROZA, THE CROWN ON HIS
HEAD HANGING BY A THREAD.

....

MAGRI HAS TO DO WELL AGAINST
THE UNKNOWN MEXICAN WHO
COMES FROM A FAMOUS FAMILY
OF FIVE BOXING BROTHERS.

THEY SAID IT WOULD LAST TWO
ROUNDS. THEY WERE HALF RIGHT –
IT LASTED FOUR.

....

NOW IT COMES TO A
SIMPLE EQUATION – WHO
CAN STAND THE HEAT.

....

MARVELLOUS ORIENTAL
PACE HE'S GOT – JUST LIKE
A BUDDHIST STATUE.

....

IT'S NOT ONE OF BRUNO'S FASTEST
WINS, BUT IT'S ONE OF THEM.

I fought Sugar Ray Robinson so **MANY TIMES THAT I'M LUCKY** I DIDN'T GET DIABETES.

JAKE 'RAGING BULL' LAMOTTA, AMERICAN BOXER

You're damn right I know where I am! I'm in Madison Square Garden getting the shit kicked out of me.

WILLIE PASTRANO, AMERICAN BOXER, ANSWERING A DOCTOR WHO WAS CHECKING ON HIS FITNESS TO CONTINUE THE FIGHT

A BOXER MAKES A COMEBACK FOR TWO REASONS: EITHER HE'S BROKE OR HE NEEDS THE MONEY.

ALAN MINTER, ENGLISH BOXER

It was a very happy fight. I was enjoying hitting him and he enjoyed getting hit.

LENNOX LEWIS, BRITISH–CANADIAN BOXER

LEATHER ON
WILLOW

WHEN YOU WIN THE TOSS – BAT.
IF YOU ARE IN DOUBT, THINK
ABOUT IT, THEN BAT. IF YOU
HAVE VERY BIG DOUBTS, CONSULT
A COLLEAGUE – THEN BAT.

W. G. GRACE, ENGLISH CRICKETER

· ·

It can't have been Gatt. Anything
he takes up to his room after
nine o'clock, he eats.

**IAN BOTHAM, ENGLISH CRICKETER, COMMENTING ON
MIKE GATTING AND THE 'BARMAID AFFAIR'**

· ·

PERSONALLY, I HAVE ALWAYS
LOOKED ON CRICKET AS
ORGANISED LOAFING.

**WILLIAM TEMPLE, NINTH ARCHBISHOP
OF CANTERBURY**

Nothing yet devised by man is worse for a sick hangover than a day's cricket in the summer sun.

MICHAEL PARKINSON, ENGLISH TV PRESENTER

....

IT REQUIRES ONE TO ASSUME SUCH INDECENT POSTURES.

OSCAR WILDE, IRISH WRITER, ON CRICKET

....

It's been a very slow and dull day, but it hasn't been boring. It's been a good, entertaining day's cricket.

TONY BENNEWORTH, AUSTRALIAN CRICKET COMMENTATOR

GOWER WORE AN EXPRESSION
OF PERMANENT PAINED
BEWILDERMENT, LIKE A MAN WHO'S
JUST STEPPED INTO A LIFT SHAFT.

MICHAEL HENDERSON, ENGLISH SPORTS JOURNALIST

· ·

My auntie could have caught
that in her pinny.

**GEOFFREY BOYCOTT, ENGLISH CRICKETER
AND COMMENTATOR**

· ·

CRICKET IS THE ONLY
GAME IN WHICH YOU CAN
ACTUALLY PUT ON WEIGHT
WHILE YOU'RE PLAYING.

TOMMY DOCHERTY, SCOTTISH FOOTBALL MANAGER

On the first day, Logie decided to chance his arm and it came off.

TREVOR BAILEY,
ENGLISH CRICKETER AND
COMMENTATOR

David Gower: Do you want
Gatting a foot wider?
Chris Cowdrey: No. He'd burst.

DURING AN INDIA V ENGLAND MATCH IN CALCUTTA

. . . .

FRED TITMUS HAS TWO SHORT
LEGS, ONE OF THEM SQUARE.

BRIAN JOHNSTON, ENGLISH CRICKET COMMENTATOR

. . . .

A snick by Jack Hobbs is a sort of
disturbance of the cosmic orderliness.

NEVILLE CARDUS, ENGLISH CRICKET WRITER

DENIS COMPTON WAS THE ONLY
PLAYER TO CALL HIS PARTNER
FOR A RUN AND WISH HIM GOOD
LUCK AT THE SAME TIME.

JOHN WARR, ENGLISH CRICKETER

....

Ken Harrington: Let's cut out
some of the quick singles.
Fred Titmus: OK, we'll cut out yours, Ken.

**DURING A MID-WICKET CONFERENCE IN
A TEST MATCH FOR ENGLAND**

....

IT'S LIKE MANCHESTER UNITED
GETTING A PENALTY AND BRYAN
ROBSON TAKING IT WITH HIS HEAD.

**DAVID LLOYD, ENGLISH CRICKETER,
ON THE REVERSE SWEEP**

Cricket is basically baseball on Valium.

ROBIN WILLIAMS, AMERICAN ACTOR

....

INNOVATIONS INVARIABLY ARE SUSPECT AND IN NO QUARTER MORE SO THAN THE CRICKET WORLD.

GILBERT JESSOP, ENGLISH CRICKETER

....

So how's your wife and my kids?

ROD MARSH, AUSTRALIAN WICKETKEEPER, TO IAN BOTHAM FROM BEHIND THE STUMPS

SHANE WARNE: I'VE BEEN WAITING TWO YEARS FOR ANOTHER CHANCE TO HUMILIATE YOU. DARYLL CULLINAN: LOOKS LIKE YOU SPENT IT ALL EATING.

THE SOUTH AFRICAN BATSMAN'S RESPONSE TO THE AUSTRALIAN BOWLER

· ·

If it had been a cheese roll, it would never have got past him.

GRAHAM GOOCH, ENGLISH CRICKETER, ON MIKE GATTING BEING BOWLED OUT AT OLD TRAFFORD

· ·

WE DIDN'T HAVE ANY METAPHORS IN MY DAY. WE DIDN'T BEAT ABOUT THE BUSH.

FRED TRUEMAN, ENGLISH CRICKETER

Pitches are like

WIVES. YOU CAN NEVER TELL HOW

THEY'RE GOING TO TURN OUT.

LEN HUTTON, ENGLISH CRICKETER

It has been said of the unseen army of the dead on their everlasting march, that when they are passing a rural cricket ground the Englishmen fall out of the ranks for a moment to lean over a gate and smile.

J. M. BARRIE, SCOTTISH WRITER

I DON'T THINK I'VE ACTUALLY DRUNK A BEER FOR 15 YEARS, EXCEPT A FEW GUINNESSES IN DUBLIN, WHERE IT'S THE LAW.

IAN BOTHAM, ENGLISH CRICKETER

Paul Harris is a buffet bowler. You just help yourself to runs.

GEOFFREY BOYCOTT, ENGLISH CRICKETER AND COMMENTATOR

· ·

HERE COMES CUNIS – HIS BOWLING, LIKE HIS NAME, NEITHER ONE THING NOR THE OTHER.

BBC TV COMMENTATOR

· ·

I'm confident they play the game in heaven. Wouldn't be heaven otherwise, would it?

PATRICK MOORE, ENGLISH ASTRONOMER

TOUCHDOWNS, SLAM DUNKS AND HOME RUNS

FOOTBALL IS NOT A CONTACT
SPORT. FOOTBALL IS A
COLLISION SPORT. DANCING
IS A CONTACT SPORT.

DUFFY DAUGHERTY, AMERICAN FOOTBALL COACH

. . . .

I told one player, 'Son, I couldn't
understand it with you. Is it ignorance
or apathy?' He said, 'Coach, I
don't know and I don't care.'

FRANK LAYDEN, AMERICAN BASKETBALL COACH

. . . .

PEOPLE ASK ME WHAT I DO IN
WINTER WHEN THERE'S NO
BASEBALL. I STARE OUT THE
WINDOW AND WAIT FOR SPRING.

ROGERS HORNSBY, AMERICAN BASEBALL PLAYER

A hot dog at the ball park is better than a steak at the Ritz.

HUMPHREY BOGART, AMERICAN ACTOR

. . . .

THE SECRET IS TO HAVE EIGHT GREAT PLAYERS AND FOUR OTHERS WHO WILL CHEER LIKE CRAZY.

JERRY TARKANIAN, AMERICAN BASKETBALL COACH

. . . .

If winning isn't everything, why do they keep score?

VINCE LOMBARDI, AMERICAN FOOTBALL COACH

WE CAN'T WIN AT HOME AND WE CAN'T WIN ON THE ROAD... I CAN'T THINK OF ANOTHER PLACE TO PLAY.

PAT WILLIAMS, AMERICAN SPORTS EXECUTIVE

· ·

I hate it. It looks like a stick-up at 7-Eleven. Five guys standing there with their hands in the air.

NORM SLOAN, AMERICAN BASKETBALL COACH, ON ZONE DEFENCE

· ·

RIGHT NOW I FEEL THAT I'VE GOT MY FEET ON THE GROUND AS FAR AS MY HEAD IS CONCERNED.

BO BELINSKY, AMERICAN BASEBALL PLAYER

I wouldn't ever set out to hurt anyone **DELIBERATELY UNLESS IT WAS, YOU KNOW, IMPORTANT –** LIKE A LEAGUE GAME OR SOMETHING.

DICK BUTKUS, AMERICAN FOOTBALL PLAYER

I'm not allowed to comment
on lousy officiating.

JIM FINKS, CANADIAN FOOTBALL PLAYER AND COACH

. . . .

WE MADE TOO MANY
WRONG MISTAKES.

YOGI BERRA, AMERICAN BASEBALL PLAYER

. . . .

We don't need refs, but I guess
white guys need something to do.

CHARLES BARKLEY, AMERICAN BASKETBALL PLAYER

OREL HERSHISER IS THE ONLY
MAJOR LEAGUE PITCHER TO
HAVE TWO CONSECUTIVE
PRONOUNS IN HIS SURNAME.

ROGER ANGELL, AMERICAN SPORTS WRITER

....

Football is an incredible game.
Sometimes it's so incredible,
it's unbelievable.

TOM LANDRY, AMERICAN FOOTBALL PLAYER

....

THERE'S NO SKILL INVOLVED.
JUST GO UP THERE AND
SWING AT THE BALL.

JOE DIMAGGIO, AMERICAN BASEBALL PLAYER

It's like déjà vu all over again.

YOGI BERRA, AMERICAN BASEBALL PLAYER

• •

MOST FOOTBALL TEAMS ARE
TEMPERAMENTAL. THAT'S
90 PER CENT TEMPER AND
10 PER CENT MENTAL.

DOUG PLANK, AMERICAN FOOTBALL COACH

• •

Baseball has the great advantage
over cricket of being ended sooner.

GEORGE BERNARD SHAW, IRISH WRITER

IF A MAN WATCHES THREE
FOOTBALL GAMES IN A ROW,
HE SHOULD BE DECLARED
LEGALLY DEAD.

ERMA BOMBECK, AMERICAN HUMORIST

The game is too long, the season is too
long and the players are too long.

JACK DOLPH, AMERICAN BASKETBALL ASSOCIATION

WE'RE NOT ATTEMPTING TO
CIRCUMCISE ANY RULES.

BILL COWHER, AMERICAN FOOTBALL COACH

He's about the size of a
lot of guys that size.

GARY CROWTON, AMERICAN FOOTBALL COACH

· ·

IF THERE'S A PILE-UP, THEY'LL HAVE TO GIVE SOME OF THE PLAYERS ARTIFICIAL INSEMINATION.

CURT GOWDY, AMERICAN SPORTSCASTER

· ·

They can't fire me because my
family buys too many tickets.

**LAVELL EDWARDS, AMERICAN FOOTBALL COACH
AND ONE OF 14 CHILDREN**

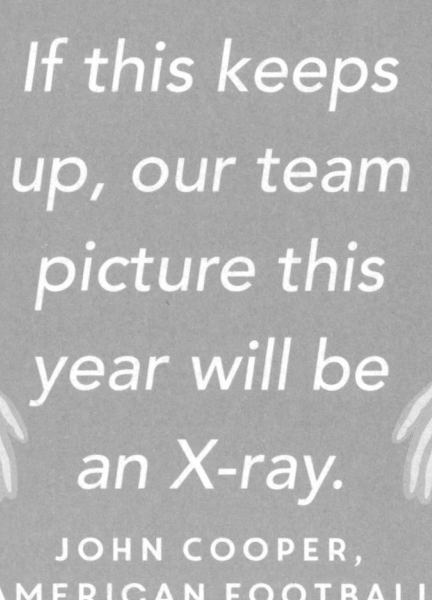

If this keeps up, our team picture this year will be an X-ray.

JOHN COOPER,
AMERICAN FOOTBALL
COACH, ON ARIZONA
STATE'S INJURY LIST

THE MOONING ALLEGATION? I'D JUST LIKE TO PUT IT BEHIND ME.

PEYTON MANNING, AMERICAN FOOTBALL PLAYER

. . . .

Baseball players are the weirdest of all. I think it's all that organ music.

**PETER GENT, AMERICAN FOOTBALL PLAYER
AND NOVELIST**

. . . .

NOT ONLY IS HE AMBIDEXTROUS, HE CAN THROW WITH EITHER HAND.

DUFFY DAUGHERTY, AMERICAN FOOTBALL COACH

I've been big ever since I was little.

WILLIAM 'THE REFRIGERATOR' PERRY, AMERICAN FOOTBALL PLAYER

. . . .

I'LL ALWAYS REMEMBER THIS AS THE NIGHT MICHAEL AND I COMBINED TO SCORE 70 POINTS.

STACEY KING, AMERICAN BASKETBALL PLAYER, AFTER MICHAEL JORDAN HAD SCORED 69 POINTS

. . . .

You guys, line up alphabetically by height.

BILL PETERSON, AMERICAN FOOTBALL COACH

MANUTE BOL IS SO TALL THAT IF HE FELL DOWN HE'D BE HALFWAY HOME.

DARRYL DAWKINS, AMERICAN BASKETBALL PLAYER, ON THE 7 FT 7 IN PLAYER

....

Gary Anderson's a great player. He ceases to amaze me every day.

RAY PERKINS, AMERICAN FOOTBALL COACH

....

WELL, THAT KIND OF PUTS THE DAMPER ON EVEN A YANKEES WIN.

PHIL RIZZUTO, AMERICAN BASEBALL PLAYER, AFTER ANNOUNCING THE DEATH OF POPE PAUL VI

An hour after the game, you want
to go out and play them again.

**ROCKY BRIDGES, AMERICAN BASEBALL PLAYER,
ON PLAYING AGAINST A TEAM FROM JAPAN**

. . . .

HATING THE NEW YORK YANKEES
IS AS AMERICAN AS APPLE PIE,
UNWED MOTHERS AND CHEATING
ON YOUR INCOME TAX.

MIKE ROYKO, AMERICAN JOURNALIST

. . . .

The underprivileged people of
the Americas play some strange
game with a bat which looks like
an overgrown rolling pin.

FRED TRUEMAN, ENGLISH CRICKETER

THERE ARE TWO KINDS OF COACHES – THOSE WHO HAVE BEEN FIRED AND THOSE WHO WILL BE FIRED.

KEN LOEFFLER, AMERICAN BASKETBALL COACH

In the great department store of life, baseball is the toy department.

ANONYMOUS

SHOOTING IS JUST LIKE TOENAILS. THEY MAY FALL OFF OCCASIONALLY, BUT YOU KNOW THEY'LL ALWAYS COME BACK.

CHARLES JOHNSON, AMERICAN BASKETBALL PLAYER

The difference between politics and baseball is that in baseball when you get caught stealing, you're out.

RON DENTINGER, AMERICAN COMEDIAN

....

I'M IN FAVOUR OF DRUG TESTS, JUST SO LONG AS THEY ARE MULTIPLE CHOICE.

KURT RAMBIS, AMERICAN BASKETBALL COACH

....

Sure, luck means a lot in football. Not having a good quarterback is bad luck.

DON SHULA, AMERICAN FOOTBALL COACH

RUNNING, JUMPING AND THROWING

AND THERE YOU SEE SEBASTIAN
COE PREPARING FOR OUR
FIRST LOOK AT HIM.

JIM ROSENTHAL, ENGLISH SPORTS PRESENTER

....

It's only jumping into a sandpit.

**JONATHAN EDWARDS, ENGLISH OLYMPIC TRIPLE
JUMPER, ON HIS WORLD RECORD TRIPLE JUMP**

....

THE DECATHLON IS NINE
MICKEY MOUSE EVENTS
AND THE 1,500 METRES.

**STEVE OVETT, ENGLISH OLYMPIC
MIDDLE DISTANCE RUNNER**

Watch the time – it gives you an indication of how fast they are running.

RON PICKERING, ENGLISH ATHLETICS COACH AND COMMENTATOR

• •

A VERY POWERFUL SET OF LUNGS, VERY MUCH HIDDEN BY THAT CHEST OF HIS.

ALAN PASCOE, ENGLISH HURDLER

• •

He's a well-balanced athlete. He has a chip on both shoulders.

DEREK REDMOND, ENGLISH RUNNER, ON LINFORD CHRISTIE

I DON'T THINK THE DISCUS WILL EVER ATTRACT INTEREST UNTIL THEY LET US START THROWING THEM AT ONE ANOTHER.

AL OERTER, AMERICAN DISCUS THROWER

· ·

I know I'm no Kim Basinger, but she can't throw a javelin.

FATIMA WHITBREAD, ENGLISH JAVELIN THROWER

· ·

BEHIND EVERY GOOD DECATHLETE, THERE'S A GOOD DOCTOR.

BILL TOOMEY, AMERICAN DECATHLETE

I just imagine all the other runners are big spiders, and then I got super scared.

USAIN BOLT, JAMAICAN SPRINTER

You don't run 26 miles at five minutes a mile on good looks and a secret recipe.

FRANK SHORTER, AMERICAN MARATHON RUNNER

· ·

WHEN I LOST MY DECATHLON
WORLD RECORD I TOOK
IT LIKE A MAN. I ONLY
CRIED FOR TEN HOURS.

DALEY THOMPSON, ENGLISH DECATHLETE

· ·

You have to be suspicious when you line up against girls with moustaches.

MAREE HOLLAND, AUSTRALIAN RUNNER

DON'T TALK ABOUT MICHAEL
JOHNSON'S STYLE. LOOK, IF
THAT GUY RAN WITH HIS
FINGERS UP HIS BUM HE COULD
STILL RUN 42 SECONDS.

ROGER BLACK, ENGLISH RUNNER AND COMMENTATOR

Running for money doesn't make
you run fast. It makes you run first.

BEN JIPCHO, KENYAN RUNNER

IF YOU WANT TO RUN A MILE,
THEN RUN A MILE. IF YOU
WANT TO EXPERIENCE ANOTHER
LIFE, RUN A MARATHON.

EMIL ZATOPEK, CZECH RUNNER

If you want to know what you'll look like in ten years, look in the mirror after you've run a marathon.

ANONYMOUS

. . . .

I WENT THROUGH A STAGE OF FEELING AWFUL TO ONE OF FEELING TERRIBLE. ONCE I STARTED TO FEEL TERRIBLE I WAS OK.

STEVE OVETT, ENGLISH RUNNER

. . . .

Scientists have proven that it's impossible to long-jump 30 feet, but I don't listen to that kind of talk.

CARL LEWIS, AMERICAN ATHLETE

If you make one mistake, it
can result in a vasectomy.

MARK ROWLAND, ENGLISH STEEPLECHASER

· ·

IF GOD INVENTED MARATHONS
TO KEEP PEOPLE FROM DOING
ANYTHING MORE STUPID, THE
TRIATHLON MUST HAVE TAKEN
HIM COMPLETELY BY SURPRISE.

P. Z. PEARCE, AMERICAN SPORTS PHYSICIAN

· ·

Linford Christie, the generously
beloined sprint supremo.

PUNCH MAGAZINE

I became a great runner because if **YOU'RE A KID IN LEEDS AND YOUR NAME IS SEBASTIAN** YOU'VE GOT TO BECOME A GREAT RUNNER.

SEBASTIAN COE, ENGLISH RUNNER

IF THIS NEW METHOD IS ACCEPTED I WILL PERSONALLY BREAK MY JAVELIN IN HALF AND USE IT AS A SUPPORT FOR MY TOMATO PLANTS.

DANA ZÁTOPKOVÁ, CZECH JAVELIN THROWER, ON NEWS OF A NEW THROWING STYLE

....

Steve Ovett, Sebastian Coe, Steve Cram – the vanguard of our cream.

RON PICKERING, ENGLISH ATHLETICS COACH AND COMMENTATOR

....

HE LOOKS LIKE THE LOVE CHILD OF GRACE JONES AND PAUL REVERE.

TONY KORNHEISER, AMERICAN SPORTS WRITER, ON CARL LEWIS'S SHORT-LIVED PONYTAIL

DAVID COLEMAN

English sports commentator David Coleman covered 11 Olympic Games for the BBC between 1960 and 2000, becoming the first broadcaster to receive the Olympic Award for 'distinguished contribution to the Olympic Movement'. He was just as well known for his priceless on-air gaffes, since immortalised as 'Colemanballs'. Here is a selection worthy of the name.

IT'S A BATTLE WITH HIMSELF
AND WITH THE TICKING FINGER
OF THE CLOCK.

. . . .

AND WITH ALPHABETICAL IRONY
NIGERIA FOLLOWS NEW ZEALAND.

. . . .

THE REPUBLIC OF CHINA – BACK
IN THE OLYMPIC GAMES FOR THE
FIRST TIME.

. . . .

IN A MOMENT, WE HOPE TO
SEE THE POLE-VAULT OVER
THE SATELLITE.

SOME NAMES TO LOOK FORWARD TO HERE – PERHAPS IN THE FUTURE.

....

HE'S 31 THIS YEAR. LAST YEAR HE WAS 30.

....

THE LATE START IS DUE TO THE TIME.

....

AND THE LINE-UP FOR THE FINAL OF THE WOMEN'S 400-METRES HURDLES INCLUDES THREE RUSSIANS, TWO EAST GERMANS, A POLE, A SWEDE AND A FRENCHMAN.

WE ESTIMATE, AND THIS ISN'T AN ESTIMATION, THAT GRETE WAITZ IS 80 SECONDS BEHIND.

....

THAT'S THE FASTEST TIME EVER RUN – BUT IT'S NOT AS FAST AS THE WORLD RECORD.

....

THIS IS A YOUNG MAN WHO IS ONLY 25, AND YOU HAVE TO SAY, HE HAS ANSWERED EVERY QUESTION THAT HAS EVER BEEN ASKED.

....

HE IS ACCELERATING ALL THE TIME. THAT LAST LAP WAS RUN IN 64 SECONDS AND THE ONE BEFORE IN 62.

You have to forget your last marathon before you try another. Your mind can't know what's coming.

FRANK SHORTER, AMERICAN MARATHON RUNNER

· ·

THE AMERICANS SOWED THE SEED, AND NOW THEY HAVE REAPED THE WHIRLWIND.

SEBASTIAN COE, ENGLISH RUNNER

· ·

I am still looking for shoes that will make running on streets feel like running barefoot across the bosoms of maidens.

DAVE BROSNAN, IRISH RUNNER

SOMETHING
A BIT FISHY

ANGLING IS EXTREMELY TIME-
CONSUMING. THAT'S SORT
OF THE WHOLE POINT.

THOMAS McGUANE, AMERICAN AUTHOR

....

Fishing is the sport of drowning worms.

ANONYMOUS

....

ANY MAN WHO PITS HIS
INTELLIGENCE AGAINST A FISH
AND LOSES, HAS IT COMING.

JOHN STEINBECK, AMERICAN WRITER

The formal term for a collection of fishermen is an exaggeration of anglers.

HENRY BEARD, AMERICAN HUMORIST

• •

FISHING IS SUCH GREAT FUN, I HAVE OFTEN FELT, THAT IT REALLY OUGHT TO BE DONE IN BED.

ROBERT TRAVER, AMERICAN LAWYER AND AUTHOR

• •

Fishing is a jerk on one end of the line waiting for a jerk on the other end of the line.

MARK TWAIN, AMERICAN WRITER

FLY FISHING MAY BE A VERY
PLEASANT AMUSEMENT; BUT
ANGLING OR FLOAT FISHING I CAN
ONLY COMPARE TO A STICK AND
A STRING, WITH A WORM AT ONE
END AND A FOOL AT THE OTHER.

SAMUEL JOHNSON, ENGLISH WRITER

• •

There is no taking trout in dry breeches.

MIGUEL DE CERVANTES, SPANISH WRITER

ALL YOU NEED TO BE A FISHERMAN IS PATIENCE AND A WORM.

HERB SHRINER, AMERICAN HUMORIST

· ·

I fish, therefore I don't golf.

BILLY CONNOLLY, SCOTTISH COMEDIAN

· ·

GOOD FISHING IS A MATTER OF TIMING. YOU HAVE TO GET THERE YESTERDAY.

MILTON BERLE, AMERICAN COMEDIAN AND ACTOR

*Our tradition is
that of the first man*

WHO SNEAKED
AWAY TO THE
CREEK WHEN

THE TRIBE DID
NOT REALLY
NEED FISH.

RODERICK HAIG-BROWN,
CANADIAN WRITER AND
CONSERVATIONIST

A trout in the pot is better
than a salmon in the sea.

IRISH PROVERB

. . . .

THERE'S A REASON THEY CALL IT
'FISHING' AND NOT 'CATCHING'.

ANONYMOUS

. . . .

Of all the liars among mankind, the
fisherman is the most trustworthy.

WILLIAM SHERWOOD FOX, AMERICAN ACADEMIC

THERE'S A FINE LINE BETWEEN
FISHING AND STANDING ON
THE SHORE LIKE AN IDIOT.

STEVEN WRIGHT, AMERICAN COMEDIAN

• •

For at least the last 275 years the
honesty of fishermen has been
somewhat questionable.

ARTHUR RANSOME, ENGLISH WRITER

• •

THE ONLY REASON I EVER
PLAYED GOLF IN THE FIRST
PLACE WAS SO I COULD AFFORD
TO HUNT AND FISH.

SAM SNEAD, AMERICAN GOLFER

In cross-examination, as in fishing, nothing is more ungainly than a fisherman pulled into the water by his catch.

LOUIS NIZER, AMERICAN LAWYER

• •

GOOD THINGS COME TO THOSE WHO BAIT.

ANONYMOUS

• •

Anglers make gentle and inoffensive creatures sound like wounded buffalo and man-eating tigers.

RODERICK HAIG-BROWN, CANADIAN WRITER AND CONSERVATIONIST

THE TWO BEST TIMES TO FISH ARE WHEN IT'S RAINING AND WHEN IT ISN'T.

PATRICK F. McMANUS, AMERICAN HUMORIST

· ·

It's a pretty good rule never to show a favourite spot to any fisherman you wouldn't trust with your wife.

ROBERT TRAVER, AMERICAN WRITER

· ·

BRAGGING MAY NOT BRING HAPPINESS, BUT NO MAN THAT EVER CAUGHT A LARGE AMOUNT OF FISH GOES HOME THROUGH AN ALLEY.

ANN LANDERS, AMERICAN COLUMNIST

The books all say that barracuda
rarely eat people, but very
few barracuda can read.

DAVE BARRY, AMERICAN AUTHOR AND COLUMNIST

. . . .

LAST YEAR I WENT FISHING
WITH SALVADOR DALÍ. HE WAS
USING A DOTTED LINE AND
CAUGHT EVERY OTHER FISH.

STEVEN WRIGHT, AMERICAN COMEDIAN

. . . .

There is no use in your walking five
miles to fish when you can depend on
being just as unsuccessful near home.

MARK TWAIN, AMERICAN WRITER

I LOVE FISHING. IT'S TRANSCENDENTAL MEDITATION WITH A PUNCHLINE.

BILLY CONNOLLY, SCOTTISH COMEDIAN

· ·

Carpe Diem does not mean 'Fish of the Day'.

ANONYMOUS

· ·

WANTED: GOOD WOMAN WHO CAN COOK, SEW, CLEAN FISH, HAS BOAT AND MOTOR. SEND PHOTO OF BOAT AND MOTOR.

OLD FISHING SIGN

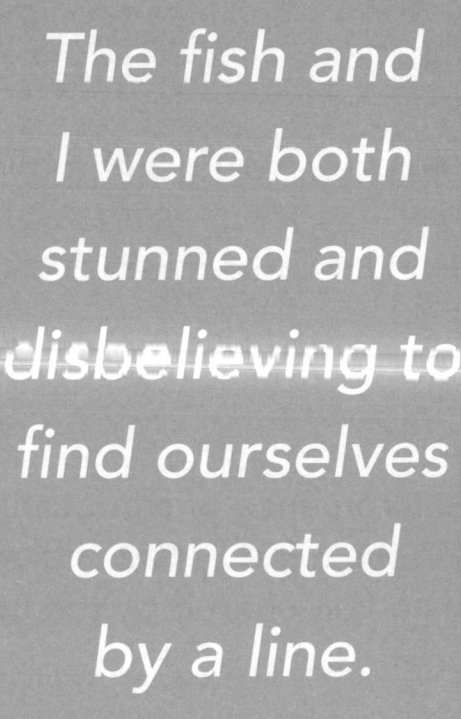

*The fish and
I were both
stunned and
disbelieving to
find ourselves
connected
by a line.*

WILLIAM HUMPHREY,
AMERICAN WRITER

Your first trout is like your first
love. You never forget it!

JIMMY D. MOORE, AMERICAN WRITER AND HUMORIST

....

FLY FISHING MAY BE A SPORT
INVENTED BY INSECTS WITH
FLY FISHERMEN AS BAIT.

P. J. O'ROURKE, AMERICAN WRITER AND HUMORIST

....

All the romance of trout fishing
exists in the mind of the angler and
is in no way shared by the fish.

HAROLD F. BLAISDELL, AMERICAN ANGLING WRITER

MANY MEN GO FISHING ALL THEIR
LIVES WITHOUT KNOWING IT
IS NOT FISH THEY ARE AFTER.

HENRY DAVID THOREAU, AMERICAN WRITER

Sometimes I do like a couple of
cooperative fish of frying size.

JOHN STEINBECK, AMERICAN WRITER

CALLING FISHING A HOBBY IS LIKE
CALLING BRAIN SURGERY A JOB.

PAUL SCHULLERY, AMERICAN NATURALIST
AND WRITER

GOING A
BIT POTTY

Now that cue arm is in perfect rhythm with his thinking.

JOHN PULLMAN, ENGLISH SNOOKER PLAYER AND COMMENTATOR

. . . .

I AM SPEAKING FROM A DESERTED AND VIRTUALLY EMPTY CRUCIBLE THEATRE.

DAVID VINE, ENGLISH SPORTS COMMENTATOR

. . . .

If I had to make the choice between staying married and playing snooker, snooker would win.

RAY REARDON, WELSH SNOOKER PLAYER

HE HAS TO STAY LEVEL, OR ONE
FRAME BEHIND; THAT'S THE
ONLY WAY HE CAN BEAT HIM.

DENNIS TAYLOR, NORTHERN IRISH SNOOKER PLAYER

From this position you've got to fancy
either yourself or your opponent winning.

KIRK STEVENS, CANADIAN SNOOKER PLAYER

STEVE DAVIS IS TRAILING BY
ONE FRAME, SO THE PRESSURE
IS BALANCED ON HIM.

**REX WILLIAMS, ENGLISH SNOOKER AND
BILLIARDS PLAYER**

But there was still the big prize money, hanging there like a carrot waiting to be picked.

DAVID VINE,
ENGLISH SPORTS
COMMENTATOR

I've always said the difference between winning and losing is nothing at all.

TERRY GRIFFITHS, WELSH SNOOKER PLAYER

....

JOHN SPENCER CAN'T REALLY AFFORD TO GO 5–1 DOWN AT SUCH AN EARLY STAGE.

JACK KARNEHM, ENGLISH SNOOKER COMMENTATOR

....

Just enough points here for Tony to pull the cat out of the fire.

RAY EDMONDS, ENGLISH SNOOKER AND BILLIARDS PLAYER

THAT SAID, THE INEVITABLE
FAILED TO HAPPEN.

JOHN PULLMAN, ENGLISH SNOOKER PLAYER
AND COMMENTATOR

....

Suddenly, Alex Higgins was 7–0 down.

DAVID VINE, ENGLISH SPORTS COMMENTATOR

....

A LOT OF SNOOKER PLAYERS ARE
TOO INTENSE AND SERIOUS. I
WANT TO BE LIKE BILLY THE KID.

RONNIE O'SULLIVAN, ENGLISH SNOOKER PLAYER

TED LOWE

The voice of snooker on the BBC for almost 40 years was English commentator Ted Lowe, known to his millions of fans as 'Whispering Ted'. His knowledge of the sport was legendary, but, like all great sports commentators, when he got it wrong, he really got it wrong.

AND GRIFFITHS HAS LOOKED AT
THAT BLUE FOUR TIMES NOW, AND
IT STILL HASN'T MOVED.

....

A LITTLE PALE IN THE FACE, BUT
THEN HIS NAME IS WHITE.

....

THE FORMALITIES ARE OVER
AND IT'S DOWN TO BUSINESS,
STEVE DAVIS NOW ADJUSTING
HIS SOCKS.

....

AND JIMMY'S POTTING
IS LITERALLY DOING THE
COMMENTARY HERE.

THAT'S INCHES AWAY FROM BEING MILLIMETRE PERFECT.

....

THIS YOUNG MAN JIMMY WHITE CELEBRATED HIS TWENTY-SECOND BIRTHDAY LITERALLY FOUR DAYS AGO.

....

THERE IS, I BELIEVE, A TIME LIMIT FOR PLAYING A SHOT. BUT I THINK IT'S TRUE TO SAY THAT NOBODY KNOWS WHAT THAT LIMIT IS.

THAT POT PUTS THE GAME
BEYOND REPROACH.

....

JIMMY WHITE HAS THAT
WONDERFUL GIFT OF BEING
ABLE TO POINT HIS CUE WHERE
HE IS LOOKING.

....

STEVE, WITH HIS SIP OF WATER,
PART OF HIS MAKE-UP.

....

HE'S COMPLETELY DISAPPEARED.
HE'S GONE BACK TO HIS DRESSING
ROOM; NOBODY KNOWS WHERE
HE HAS GONE.

HE'S LUCKY IN ONE SENSE AND
LUCKY IN THE OTHER.

....

OH, AND THAT'S A BRILLIANT SHOT.
THE ODD THING IS, HIS MUM'S NOT
VERY KEEN ON SNOOKER.

....

HIGGINS FIRST ENTERED THE
CHAMPIONSHIP TEN YEARS AGO.
THAT WAS FOR THE FIRST TIME,
OF COURSE.

....

AND IT IS MY GUESS THAT
STEVE DAVIS WILL TRY TO
SCORE AS MANY POINTS AS
HE CAN THIS FRAME.

I like playing in Sheffield. It's

FULL OF MELANCHOLY,

HAPPY-GO-LUCKY PEOPLE.

ALEX HIGGINS, NORTHERN IRISH
SNOOKER PLAYER

I suppose the charisma bypass operation was a big disappointment in my life.

STEVE DAVIS, ENGLISH SNOOKER PLAYER, MUSING ON CRITICISM OF HIS 'BORING' PERSONALITY

....

THE MATCH HAS GRADUALLY AND SUDDENLY COME TO A CLIMAX.

DAVID VINE, ENGLISH SPORTS COMMENTATOR

....

Frankly, I'd rather have a drink with Idi Amin.

ALEX HIGGINS, NORTHERN IRISH SNOOKER PLAYER, ON 'INTERESTING' STEVE DAVIS

THE RUDE
BITS

THERE GOES JUANTORENA DOWN THE BACK STRAIGHT, OPENING HIS LEGS AND SHOWING HIS CLASS.

DAVID COLEMAN, ENGLISH SPORTS COMMENTATOR

....

I think the French always niggle, grabbing blokes around the balls and the eyes and that sort of thing.

TIM LANE, AUSTRALIAN RUGBY PLAYER AND COACH

....

AH, ISN'T THAT NICE, THE WIFE OF THE CAMBRIDGE PRESIDENT IS KISSING THE COX OF THE OXFORD CREW.

HARRY CARPENTER, ENGLISH SPORTS PRESENTER, ON THE UNIVERSITY BOAT RACE

You don't like to see hookers going down on players like that.

MURRAY MEXTED, NEW ZEALAND RUGBY PLAYER AND COMMENTATOR

· ·

THE BEST WAY TO A FISHERMAN'S HEART IS THROUGH HIS FLY.

ANONYMOUS

· ·

This is the second most exciting indoor sport, and the other one shouldn't have spectators.

DICK VERTLEIB, AMERICAN BASKETBALL COACH

I'M NOT A BIG SPORTS FAN,
BUT I LOVE IT WHEN THEY
'SLAM DUNK'. THAT'S SEXY.

EMMA BUNTON, ENGLISH SINGER

My girlfriend boos me when we make
love because she knows it turns me on.

HECTOR CAMACHO, PUERTO RICAN BOXER

I DON'T CARE FOR SEX. I FIND
IT AN EMBARRASSING, DULL
EXERCISE. I PREFER SPORTS,
WHERE YOU CAN WIN.

NORM MACDONALD, CANADIAN ACTOR

And this is Gregoriava from Bulgaria. I saw her snatch this morning and it was amazing!

PAT GLENN,
WEIGHTLIFTING
COMMENTATOR

Plainly no way has yet been found to stop long-jump commentaries sounding like naughty stories after lights-out in the dorm. 'Ooooh! It's enormous. It was so long!'

RUSSELL DAVIES, WELSH JOURNALIST AND BROADCASTER

WHY CAN'T YOU LET PLAYERS LIFT UP THEIR SHIRTS? WHO IS IT DISRESPECTING? WHAT'S WRONG WITH LETTING A LOAD OF YOUNG LADIES SEE A GOOD-LOOKING LAD TAKE HIS SHIRT OFF?

IAN HOLLOWAY, ENGLISH FOOTBALL MANAGER

When I first heard about Viagra,
I thought it was a new player
Chelsea had just signed.

TONY BANKS, BRITISH SPORTS MINISTER

· ·

DESIRE, IT'S A GREAT WORD.
I OFTEN USE THE WORD
'HORNY' WITH MY PLAYERS.

**LOUIS VAN GAAL, DUTCH FOOTBALL MANAGER,
ON MANCHESTER UNITED**

· ·

I think it's a great idea to talk during
sex, as long as it's about snooker.

STEVE DAVIS, ENGLISH SNOOKER PLAYER

WELCOME TO LEICESTER, WHERE
THE CAPTAIN RAY ILLINGWORTH
HAS JUST RELIEVED HIMSELF
AT THE PAVILION END.

BRIAN JOHNSTON, ENGLISH CRICKET COMMENTATOR

....

He's the kind of player you expect to see
emerging from a ruck with the remains
of a jockstrap between his teeth.

TONY O'REILLY, IRISH RUGBY PLAYER

....

THERE'S NOTHING THAT A TIGHT
FORWARD LIKES MORE THAN A
LOOSIE RIGHT UP HIS BACKSIDE.

**MURRAY MEXTED, NEW ZEALAND RUGBY PLAYER
AND COMMENTATOR**

I don't think there is anything sexier

THAN JUST STANDING IN WADERS WITH

A FLY ROD.
I JUST LOVE IT.

LINDA HAMILTON,
AMERICAN ACTRESS

It's tough for a natural
hooker to give it up.

IAN CHAPPELL, AUSTRALIAN CRICKETER

· ·

LINFORD CHRISTIE HAS A
HABIT OF PULLING IT OUT
WHEN IT MATTERS MOST.

DAVID COLEMAN, ENGLISH SPORTS COMMENTATOR

· ·

I suppose doing a love scene with
Raquel Welch roughly corresponds
to scoring a century before lunch.

OLIVER REED, ENGLISH ACTOR

Some weeks Nick likes to use Fanny. Other weeks he prefers to do it by himself.

KEN BROWN, SCOTTISH GOLFER, ON GOLFER NICK FALDO AND HIS CADDIE FANNY SUNESSON

....

SPENCER'S RUNNING ACROSS THE FIELD CALLING OUT: 'COME INSIDE ME! COME INSIDE ME!'

MURRAY MEXTED, NEW ZEALAND RUGBY PLAYER AND COMMENTATOR

....

The bowler's Holding, the batsman's Willey.

BRIAN JOHNSTON, ENGLISH CRICKET COMMENTATOR

JIMMY WHITE HAS POPPED OUT
TO THE TOILET TO COMPOSE
HIMSELF FOR THE FINAL PUSH.

**STEVE DAVIS, ENGLISH SNOOKER PLAYER
AND COMMENTATOR**

It was an excellent performance in
the field marred only when Harris
dropped Crapp in the outfield.

BBC CRICKET COMMENTARY

HE'S USUALLY A GOOD PULLER, BUT
HE COULDN'T GET IT UP THAT TIME.

**RICHIE BENAUD, AUSTRALIAN CRICKETER
AND COMMENTATOR**

I've never got to the
bottom of streaking.

**JONATHAN AGNEW, ENGLISH CRICKETER
AND COMMENTATOR**

. . . .

FISHING SEEMS TO BE
DIVIDED, LIKE SEX, INTO THREE
UNEQUAL PARTS: ANTICIPATION,
RECOLLECTION AND, BETWEEN
THEM, ACTUAL PERFORMANCE.

ARNOLD GINGRICH, AMERICAN JOURNALIST

. . . .

Cricket is indescribable. How do
you describe an orgasm?

**GREG MATTHEWS, AUSTRALIAN CRICKETER
AND COMMENTATOR**

YES, WE WERE ALL NAKED TOGETHER AT TIMES, BUT SO WHAT? THE ONLY CHAPS WHO WERE PERHAPS A BIT SHY INITIALLY WERE THOSE WITH SMALL WILLIES.

ANONYMOUS SOUTH AFRICAN RUGBY PLAYER COMMENTING ON THEIR 2003 WORLD CUP TRAINING CAMP

Cornering is like bringing a woman to climax.

JACKIE STEWART, SCOTTISH RACING DRIVER

JULIAN DICKS IS EVERYWHERE. IT'S LIKE THEY'VE GOT 11 DICKS ON THE FIELD.

METRO RADIO COMMENTARY

Yelena Isinbayeva loves to get hold of a stiff pole – soft ones are no good to her.

PAUL DICKENSON, ENGLISH HAMMER THROWER AND SPORTS COMMENTATOR, ON THE RUSSIAN POLE-VAULTER

· ·

I DON'T LIKE THIS NEW LAW, BECAUSE AS SOON AS YOU SEE A MAN ON THE GROUND YOUR FIRST INSTINCT IS TO GO DOWN ON HIM.

MURRAY MEXTED, NEW ZEALAND RUGBY PLAYER AND COMMENTATOR

· ·

Professional coaching is a man trying to get your legs close together when other men have spent a lifetime trying to get them wider apart.

RACHAEL HEYHOE FLINT, ENGLISH CRICKETER AND JOURNALIST

NEIL HARVEY'S AT SLIP,
WITH HIS LEGS WIDE APART,
WAITING FOR A TICKLE.

BRIAN JOHNSTON, ENGLISH CRICKET COMMENTATOR

• •

Fly fishing is like sex: everyone thinks
there is more than there is, and that
everyone is getting more than their share.

HENRY KANEMOTO, AMERICAN ANGLER

• •

AND LATER WE WILL HAVE ACTION
FROM THE MEN'S COCKLESS PAIRS.

**SUE BARKER, ENGLISH TENNIS PLAYER
AND SPORTS PRESENTER**

There's a great advantage to
be able to swim inside the legs
of the man in front of you.

DAVID WILKIE, SCOTTISH SWIMMER

• •

I WOULD RATHER WATCH A
MAN AT HIS TOILET THAN
ON A CRICKET FIELD.

ROBERT MORLEY, ENGLISH ACTOR

• •

There's nothing new you can say
about Linford Christie – except, he's
slow and he's got a small penis.

NICK HANCOCK, ENGLISH TV PRESENTER

SPORT FOR
THE LESS
ENTHUSIASTIC

JOGGING IS FOR PEOPLE WHO AREN'T INTELLIGENT ENOUGH TO WATCH TELEVISION.

VICTORIA WOOD, ENGLISH COMEDIAN

....

Curling is just housework on ice.

LINDA SMITH, ENGLISH COMEDIAN

....

HUMILIATION IS THAT AWKWARD MOMENT WHEN YOU'RE WEARING NIKES AND YOU JUST CAN'T DO IT.

ANONYMOUS

The only reason I would take up jogging is so that I could hear heavy breathing again.

ERMA BOMBECK, AMERICAN HUMORIST

· ·

BIOGRAPHY, LIKE BIG GAME HUNTING, IS ONE OF THE RECOGNISED FORMS OF SPORT, AND IT IS AS UNFAIR AS ONLY SPORT CAN BE.

PHILIP GUEDALLA, ENGLISH HISTORIAN AND WRITER

· ·

The only weights I lift are my dogs.

OLIVIA NEWTON-JOHN, AUSTRALIAN SINGER

IF MORNING JOGGERS KNEW
HOW TEMPTING THEY LOOKED
TO MORNING MOTORISTS,
THEY WOULD STAY HOME
AND DO SIT-UPS.

RITA RUDNER, AMERICAN COMEDIAN

• •

I hate all sports as rabidly as a person
who likes sports hates common sense.

H. L. MENCKEN, AMERICAN JOURNALIST AND CRITIC

• •

THE BALL IS MAN'S MOST
DISASTROUS INVENTION, NOT
EXCLUDING THE WHEEL.

ROBERT MORLEY, ENGLISH ACTOR

*My doctor told me
that jogging could*

ADD YEARS
TO MY LIFE...

I FEEL TEN YEARS
OLDER ALREADY.

MILTON BERLE,
AMERICAN COMEDIAN

Swimming isn't a sport. It's just a way to keep from drowning.

GEORGE CARLIN, AMERICAN COMEDIAN

. . . .

THE WINTER OLYMPICS ARE NOTHING MORE THAN 40 KINDS OF SLIDING.

DARA Ó BRIAIN, IRISH COMEDIAN

. . . .

The first time I see a jogger smiling, I'll consider it.

JOAN RIVERS, AMERICAN COMEDIAN

I DON'T JOG. IF I DIE I
WANT TO BE SICK.

ABE LEMONS, AMERICAN BASKETBALL COACH

....

There is something wrong with a society
that drives a car to a workout in the gym.

**BILL NYE, AMERICAN SCIENCE EDUCATOR
AND COMEDIAN**

....

THE TROUBLE WITH JOGGING IS
THAT BY THE TIME YOU REALISE
YOU'RE NOT IN SHAPE FOR IT,
IT'S TOO FAR TO WALK BACK.

FRANKLIN P. JONES, AMERICAN JOURNALIST

Of course I have played outdoor games. I once played dominoes in an open-air cafe in Paris.

OSCAR WILDE,
IRISH WRITER

If you want me to go running with you, I'm going to need some motivation – like a clown chasing us with a bloody knife and margaritas at the finish line.

ANONYMOUS

....

I ONCE JOGGED TO THE ASHTRAY.

**WILL SELF, ENGLISH WRITER, WHEN ASKED
IF HE EXERCISED**

COME
AGAIN?

I never predict anything
and I never will do.

PAUL GASCOIGNE, ENGLISH FOOTBALLER

....

HE WAS A GREAT TENNIS
PLAYER, RATHER LIKE A CHESS
PLAYER, ALWAYS TRYING TO
THREAD THE BALL THROUGH
THE EYE OF A NEEDLE.

TALK RADIO COMMENTARY

....

Ingemar Johansson is a leviathan
with a strangler's hands and a smile
like the beam of a lighthouse.

**LOUIS T. STANLEY, ENGLISH JOURNALIST,
ON THE SWEDISH BOXER**

THERE IS NO TALK, NONE SO WITTY AND BRILLIANT, THAT IS SO GOOD AS CRICKET TALK, WHEN MEMORY SHARPENS MEMORY, AND THE DEAD LIVE AGAIN – THE REGRETTED, THE FORGOTTEN – AND THE OLD HAPPY DAYS OF BURNED-OUT JUNES REVIVE.

ANDREW LANG, SCOTTISH WRITER

. . . .

How can the ladies hurt their delicate fingers, and even bring them to blisters, holding a nasty, filthy bat? How can their sweet, delicate fingers bear the jarrings attending the catching of a dirty ball?

JOHN SACKVILLE, 3RD DUKE OF DORSET, ON THE PROPOSITION THAT WOMEN BE ALLOWED TO PLAY CRICKET

This is the third week the fish seem to be getting away from British tennis players.

GERALD WILLIAMS,
BRITISH TENNIS
COMMENTATOR

CAPITAL GAIN – SMART SPORT – FINE EXERCISE – VERY.

CHARLES DICKENS, ENGLISH WRITER, ON CRICKET

. . . .

The breakfast of champions is not cereal, it's the opposition.

NICK SEITZ, AMERICAN GOLF WRITER

. . . .

I AM A GREAT GOLFER. I JUST HAVEN'T PLAYED THE GAME YET.

MUHAMMAD ALI, AMERICAN BOXER

Baseball and cricket are beautiful and highly stylised medieval war substitutes, chess made flesh, a mixture of proud chivalry.

JOHN FOWLES, ENGLISH NOVELIST

. . . .

HE'S BEEN IN A DIFFERENT CLASS IN TRAINING AND ON THE PITCH. HE'S A LOVELY GUY AND IF I HAD A DAUGHTER I'D LET HER MARRY HIM. BUT I HAVEN'T GOT A DAUGHTER AND HE'S ALREADY MARRIED.

TERRY BUTCHER, ENGLISH FOOTBALL MANAGER

Here was English cricket's Messiah, preceded by Ian Botham's shaggy John the Baptist.

JOHN DUGDALE, ENGLISH JOURNALIST, ON GRAEME HICK

....

JOHN CONTEH HAS A NECK LIKE A STATELY HOME STAIRCASE.

TOM DAVIES, ENGLISH BOXER

....

I have ten pairs of trainers – one for every day of the week.

SAMANTHA FOX, ENGLISH GLAMOUR MODEL

THIERRY HAS BEEN ABSOLUTELY MAGICAL AND I LOVE THE WAY HE PLAYS THE GAME AND EXPRESSES HIMSELF. HE IS LIKE MERLIN THE MAGICIAN AND DR WHO ROLLED INTO ONE.

GORDON TAYLOR, ENGLISH PFA CHIEF EXECUTIVE, ON THIERRY HENRY

Lord Nelson! Lord Beaverbrook! Sir Winston Churchill! Sir Anthony Eden! Clement Attlee! Henry Cooper! Lady Diana! Maggie Thatcher – can you hear me, Maggie Thatcher? Your boys took one hell of a beating! Your boys took one hell of a beating!

BJØRGE LILLELIEN, NORWEGIAN SPORTS COMMENTATOR, AFTER NORWAY BEAT ENGLAND IN A WORLD CUP QUALIFIER

FORASMUCH AS THERE IS GREAT NOISE IN THE CITY CAUSED BY HUSTLING OVER LARGE BALLS, FROM WHICH MANY EVILS MAY ARISE, WHICH GOD FORBID, WE COMMAND AND FORBID ON BEHALF OF THE KING, ON PAIN OF IMPRISONMENT, SUCH GAME TO BE USED IN THE CITY IN FUTURE.

PROCLAMATION FROM EDWARD II IN 1314, TO PUT AN END TO FOOTBALL

I'm glad to say that this is the first Saturday in four weeks that sport will be weather-free.

DAVID COLEMAN, ENGLISH SPORTS COMMENTATOR

Had W. G. Grace

**BEEN BORN IN
ANCIENT GREECE,
THE ILIAD WOULD**

HAVE BEEN A
DIFFERENT BOOK.

BISHOP OF HEREFORD

WEIGHTLIFTERS... WHY DO THEY NEED TO WEAR LEOTARDS? REMOVAL MEN DON'T, AND THEY DO EXACTLY THE SAME JOB.

THE GUARDIAN

. . . .

I said to them last week that I'd like them to win ugly and they certainly won ugly today. That was the ugliest thing I've seen since the ugly sisters fell out of the ugly tree.

TERRY BUTCHER, ENGLISH FOOTBALL MANAGER

THERE'S NO SUCH THING AS LACK OF CONFIDENCE. YOU EITHER HAVE IT OR YOU DON'T.

ROB ANDREW, ENGLISH RUGBY PLAYER

I am the living attestation of the American dream. I am the extolment of this great nation.

DON KING, AMERICAN BOXING PROMOTER

IT WAS NOT UNLIKE WATCHING LAZARUS RISE FROM THE DEAD AND GET MOWN DOWN BY A RUNAWAY TRUCK.

IAN WOOLDRIDGE, ENGLISH SPORTS JOURNALIST, ON A NEW ZEALAND PERFORMANCE AGAINST PAKISTAN

To be a great fast bowler, you need
a big heart and a big bottom.

FRED TRUEMAN, ENGLISH CRICKETER

. . . .

YOU'VE GOT TO TAKE THE
ROUGH WITH THE SMOOTH. IT'S
LIKE LOVE AND HATE, WAR AND
PEACE, ALL THAT BOLLOCKS.

IAN WRIGHT, ENGLISH FOOTBALLER

. . . .

Next morning, England's remaining
wickets were taken quicker than a
stray fiver on the Portobello Road.

THE SUNDAY TIMES

I CAN SEE THE CARROT AT THE END OF THE TUNNEL.

STUART PEARCE, ENGLISH FOOTBALLER

....

Life is an elaborate metaphor for cricket.

MARVIN COHEN, ENGLISH WRITER

....

I'VE HAD IT. IF ANYONE SEES ME NEAR A BOAT THEY CAN SHOOT ME.

STEVE REDGRAVE, ENGLISH ROWER, SPEAKING AFTER WINNING A FOURTH OLYMPIC GOLD IN 1996 (HE WOULD WIN A FIFTH IN 2000)

I feel like dog trainer who teach dog manners and graces and just when you think dog knows how should act with nice qualities, dog make big puddle and all is wasted.

ION TIRIAC, ROMANIAN TENNIS PLAYER AND COACH, ON BEING ILIE NĂSTASE'S COACH

HARDY AMIES ONCE TOLD ME THAT THE SEXIEST THING HE HAD SEEN WAS NUNS PLAYING TENNIS.

PRUDENCE GLYNN, ENGLISH FASHION JOURNALIST

Steve Beaton, the Adonis of darts – what poise, what elegance – a true Roman gladiator with plenty of hair wax.

SID WADDELL, ENGLISH DARTS COMMENTATOR

SO YOU THINK YOU KNOW ALL ABOUT FOOTBALL

JONNO TURNER

SO YOU THINK YOU KNOW ALL ABOUT FOOTBALL

Jonno Turner

Hardback

978-1-84953-763-6

£9.99

Did you know…

- Eiður Guðjohnsen made history playing for Iceland in a friendly against Estonia in 1996 when he came on as the substitute for his own father, Arnór?

- Coventry City FC have played in the Premier League, The First, Second, Third and Fourth Divisions and Division 3 North and South?

- In recognition of their unbeaten Premier League record that year, 2003–4 winners Arsenal were presented with a special gold Premier League trophy?

Lace up your boots for this collection of mind-blowing trivia and top-tier questions about the beautiful game – and find out if you're on the ball with your football facts.

Very

BRITISH

WIT

QUIPS AND QUOTES TO SUIT
ALL MANNER OF OCCASIONS

Richard Benson